Art Is a Way of Knowing

Books by Pat B. Allen

Art Is a Spiritual Path

Art Is a Way of Knowing

Art
Is a Way of
Knowing

Pat B. Allen

Foreword by M.C. Richards

Shambhala · Boulder · 1995

For Tom and Gin

Shambhala Publications, Inc.
4720 Walnut Street
Boulder, Colorado 80301
www.shambhala.com

© 1995 by Pat B. Allen

22   21   20   19   18   17   16

Printed in the United States of America
⊗ This edition is printed on acid-free paper that meets
the American National Standards Institute z39.48 Standard.
♻ Shambhala Publications makes every effort to print on recycled
paper. For more information please visit www.shambhala.com.
Distributed in the United States by Penguin Random House LLC
and in Canada by Random House of Canada Ltd

Library of Congress Cataloging-in-Publication Data
Allen, Pat B.
   Art is a way of knowing/Pat B. Allen.
      p.   cm.
   Includes bibliographical references.
   ISBN 978-1-57062-078-2 (pbk.: alk. paper)
      1. Art therapy.   2. Art—Psychological aspects.   3. Self-
perception.   4. Imagery—Therapeutic use.   I. Title.
RC489.A7A42   1995   94-40385
700'.19—dc20   CIP

Contents

Foreword

This book is both wonderfully concrete in its methods and examples, and totally aware of the "unknowing" essential to the art process. Artwork of this kind is a way of nonintellectual knowing, through emotion and body. It evokes in the soul an intuition of selfhood—at home in the mysteries of existence, renewable through change.

This is a book I needed to reread in order to gather its harvest, for the range and depth of its content are exceptional. Allen's subject is image-making, artwork, as a way of knowing the life of the soul. She gives generous help about how to begin, materials, space, atmosphere—and then teaches us to trust the process. It is the underground river that gives us life and mobility. It takes time to make the image through clay, paint, pastels, collage, found materials, and time for the image to ripen. The art process carries us free of conscious thinking and judging. This absorption in the process is what heals. It accesses another part of oneself, where the mysteries of pain and release, grief and anger and despair, longing and hope are present. Allen's image work sustains her through experiences of death, birth, professional stress, family crises. One does this work for personal health, yes, but for the larger fabric of values in the culture as well. This fabric "only shifts incrementally, as individuals do the difficult work of changing themselves." Allen's life experience of image work helps to map the journey for us.

M. C. Richards

Preface

Images take me apart; images put me back together again, new, enlarged, with breathing room. For twenty years I have kept a record of my inner life in images, paintings, drawings, and words—sometimes haphazardly, sometimes more diligently, but continuously throughout my days as an art student, art therapist, teacher, wife, mother, and artist. I did this, I think, because I felt in a way that I didn't exist. My existence was marginal, uncompelling, because my feelings, necessary for a sense of meaning, were missing. Art making is my way of bringing soul back into my life. Soul is the place where the messiness of life is tolerated, where feelings animate the narration of life, where story exists. Soul is the place where I am replenished and can experience both gardens and graveyards. Art is my way of knowing who I am.

It is possible to give a very convincing portrayal of a life even with one's soul in exile. Only the meaning is missing. When I first began doing work with images, there were times when I thought I was insane, so unfamiliar to me was the chaos of human feeling. I have felt split off from sunlight and laughter even as I have stood in the sun and laughed with friends, and have thought no one else ever felt this way. Images have allowed me to reclaim some of what was lost in growing up, the ability to have feelings fully and in the moment. I don't believe that art cures or fixes; rather it restores the connection to soul, which is always waiting to be reclaimed.

Throughout this book I use the terms *image, image making,* and *artwork* more often than the seemingly simpler word *art*. There are value judgments inherent in the word *art* that tend to act as barriers for many people. There is good art and bad art, fine art and high art. All of these terms evoke an end product, a drawing, a painting, an object. Images, however, are a universal phenomenon that each of us experiences continuously in dreams, in our mind's eye, when we hear music or read a poem or encounter a scent that evokes a memory. We all have many internal images of our self, of those we love and those we hate. We have images of people we have never met and places we have never visited. Art making is the process of giving these images form. The marks we make in this process of giving form need not be evaluated by any outside criteria but rather by our internal sense of what is true.

Making images is a way of breaking boundaries, loosening outworn ideas, and making way for the new. It is a form of practice, through which, like any spiritual discipline, knowledge of ourselves can ripen into wisdom. Images are not always beautiful; often they are raw and mysterious. They are not always comforting but can be exhilarating, challenging, provocative, even frightening at times.

Art Is a Way of Knowing stresses the process of working with images, somewhat more than the product. Many people never attempt to make images, because what would they do with the product? Do I have to frame it? Sell it? Show it? Share it? Critique it? Develop it? Market it? Make twelve more and go to an art fair? What if I like making images; do I have to quit my job and do this all the time? Do I have to call myself an artist? Can I? As a way of knowing, art doesn't demand that you change your life any more than trying meditation demands that you shave your head and enter a monastery. How much you welcome your images and the stories they bring into your life is up to you.

I have interwoven my own story with instructions for the reader in order to show that the process is multifaceted, sometimes straightforward, sometimes not, and that it can only be learned by doing. Each person's form of art-making practice will be unique, created anew from the endless possibilities of image making.

Art Is a Way of Knowing is for anyone who wishes to contact his or her feeling, intuition, and sensing inner being and to forge a path to the river of soul that runs below everyday life, becoming more alive in the process. Teachers or other guides may be helpful along the way but are not necessary to begin. All that is necessary is the courage and curiosity to make contact with the imagination and the means to make a mark. The stories are already within you, waiting to be told.

Acknowledgments

I am grateful for the love and support of my family and many friends while writing this book. Special thanks go to those who served as angels during crucial points in the process: Evelina Weber, who read the early and tender chapters; Joan Fee, Sallie Wolf, and Pam Todd, who coaxed the manuscript along to completion; and Kendra Crossen at Shambhala for discovering the title embedded somewhere in the text as well as editing and refining the manuscript. For unwavering support of my work, challenging critique of my writing, and an enthusiastic introduction to Shambhala Publications, I thank Shaun McNiff, my generous friend and esteemed colleague.

Introduction

What I have done in my life and written about here is my direct participation in art making guided by the idea that art is a means to know the self. Art therapy, the profession I have been involved in for the past twenty years, is mostly about getting other people to know themselves through art making. I am an anomaly in that I have engaged in the process myself as much as or more than I have engaged others in it. Although I have exhibited my work from time to time, that has not been my focus. The process of using materials, struggling with their inherent qualities and limitations, has been and continues to be a wonderful arena in which to work things out.

Art therapy began as a loose collection of individuals from varied backgrounds who invented or discovered ways to use art in the service of others. Early pioneers worked among institutionalized children (Kramer 1958, 1971, 1979), psychiatric inmates (Naumburg 1966; Ulman & Dachinger 1975), and the inhabitants of state hospital back wards (McNiff 1981). Before training programs, each of these art therapists, in their own idiosyncratic ways, provided art as a voice for the unheard and forgotten. I have known and learned from all these exceptional people and for the theory and practice of art therapy, I refer the reader to their many works. I don't review the art therapy literature here nor do I cite examples from my work with clients.

Although I have studied and practiced art therapy for many years, my most significant experiences have come through using materials to discover and follow my own stream of imagery. It is the story of these images and the methods of knowing that I have used that I offer to the reader. Through art making I have solved problems, assuaged pain, faced losses and disappointments, and come to know myself deeply. For these reasons I consider making art my spiritual path. I believe this path is available to everyone and requires no "talent" beyond the talent for living inherent in us all. The gift of creativity is within each of us waiting to unfold. The results of one journey are in no way comparable to any other.

This point of view makes me something of a refugee from the world of art therapy, which has gradually developed into a profession closely allied to the field of mental health. Many art therapists began as refugees from the "art world," fleeing what had become, by the time I was in art school in the mid 1970s, the art marketplace. Art for art's sake, the doctrine of modernism, left out human empathy and stressed alienation as the hallmark of the artist. Since the 1950s, art has developed into a profession spawning whole industries which reflect the general fragmentation of work life in our society. Critics, journalists, art historians, curators, dealers, and collectors all vie for the role of the creator of meaning, while the artist stands mutely by, heroically isolated.

Art therapy seemed originally a refuge; it confirmed my need to connect with others. It seemed like work that returned to the origins of art as spiritual communication and the sacralizing of experience (Gablik 1992). But gradually art therapy, too, has embraced the ideal of professionalism. Too often art making is being coopted as just another "treatment modality" with prescribed goals and outcomes requiring predetermined meanings assigned to images. This sanitized, soulless version of art must be administered to others, interpreted by trained professionals. This sort of professionalism robs art of one of its most potent properties, the ability to dissolve boundaries and reveal our interconnectedness with one another, as well as reveal the dignity of our uniqueness.

At one time, prior to the rise of industrialism and the burgeoning of professional specialization, one way society created culture was through a rich folk art tradition. Ordinary people made objects and images to mark births and deaths, memorialize important experiences, and enhance their pleasure in living. These objects now reside in places like the Abby Aldrich Rockefeller Folk Art Museum in Williamsburg, Virginia, made precious by their scarcity. Meanwhile, our consumer culture substitutes greeting cards and craft kits for personal expression among the masses, while genuine folk art items fetch increasingly high prices as the newest segment of the art market. Art therapy pioneer Edith Kramer suggests that art as a form of therapy has arisen to fill the void created by the depleting nature of contemporary work in tandem with the demise of the participatory folk art tradition and the rise of spectator recreation. Art as a way of knowing offers a path back to direct participation in life.

Suzi Gablik in *The Reenchantment of Art* describes how some artists are beginning to reject modernist and postmodernist ideals of alienation and isolation in favor of art that is empathic, connected, and alive. She says: "The necessity for art to transform its goals and become accountable in the planetary whole is incompatible with aesthetic attitudes still predicated on the late-modernist assumption that art has no 'useful' role to play in the larger sphere of things" (1991:7).

There are a number of individuals whose work I admire and have been sustained by during my own development. Each recognizes the "useful" role art can play both for the individual and for society. Florence Cane, author of *The Artist in Each of Us* (1951), created methods through which her students learned to access authentic personal imagery. She was among the first visual artists to recognize the paramount role of bodily experience and the integrating effect of art on the mental, physical, emotional, and spiritual totality of a human being. Her work offered to ordinary people the methods adapted by her sister, art therapist Margaret Naumburg, in her work with individuals suffering mental illness.

Elizabeth Layton, who believed that drawing saved her life (Mid-America Arts Alliance 1984), began to make contour drawings late in life. She frequently made self-portraits to come to terms with a life-long depression that had remained untouched by medication and therapy. Layton, who died recently, never sold her drawings. She felt that their value derived from the effect of the whole series on the viewer. Bob Ault, an art therapist and friend of Layton's, has created a course based on her contour drawing technique and has studied the psychological impact of contour drawing.

Edward Adamson opened a studio in a British mental hospital in 1946. In the foreword to Adamson's *Art as Healing,* Anthony Stevens writes that the patients there found a haven of peace and sanity, where they could examine their private world and give it some form of expression—forms which Adamson, with abundant sensitivity and compassion, knew how to receive. (Adamson 1984)

Bolek Greczynski, founder and director of the Living Museum at Creedmore Psychiatric Hospital, in Queens, New York, has created a studio and museum that confounds all stereotypes of the art of people with mental illness while simultaneously challenging the contemporary art world with provocative shows by inmates outside the institution's walls (Hollander 1993). Tim Rollins, an artist and teacher, rejects the concept of artist as isolate. Along with adolescents in the impoverished Bronx, Rollins and K.O.S., or Kids of Survival, as they named their group, create extraordinary collaborative work based on classics of literature as a way to understand and express the meaning of the literature.

Henry Schaefer-Simmern (1948) carried out art programs among varied groups, including delinquents, the developmentally disabled, and a group of business people, which showed clearly that authentic artistic expression will unfold in a natural progression in anyone given the opportunity to make art. His methods also proved that the artistic expression would develop in complexity, interest, and personal meaning over time without invasive teaching of concepts or contrived exercises. Schaefer-Simmern's students found that as they developed their personal aesthetic they became sensitized to the chaos and disorder in their urban surroundings and less willing to tolerate the unharmonious clash of forms they encountered in daily life. Like Florence Cane, Schaefer-Simmern saw the engagement in creative endeavor as a means for people to realize wholeness and begin to deal with problems larger than their own personal experience, becoming ultimately an instrument of social change.

Among art therapists, Shaun McNiff (1992) has been a consistent voice for keeping personal, authentic art making as a key to soul rather than as clinical data. His works trace the lineage of art therapy back to its spiritual rather than psychiatric forebears.

Even more important than any published literature have been my fellow travelers, other art therapists and artists, workshop participants, and clients, who find art making a crucial and sustaining part of life and who have shared my images and generously shared theirs with me. These include my partners in the Open Studio Project, Dayna Block and Debbie Gadiel, as well as Carole Isaacs, Evelina Weber, Dan Anthon, Don Seiden, Shaun McNiff, Michael Franklin, Janis Timm-Bottos, David Henley, and my frequent partners in despair and chagrin at art therapy, my fellow doom-and-gloom girls, Cathy Malchiodi and Mariagnese Cattanco. From their personal commitment to authenticity all of those mentioned have enlarged my view of what it means to be creative and to make art.

This work, then, is directed to those who suspect there is much within themselves to know and who can imagine that much pleasure can be found in color, shape, form, and image. It is an invitation to those seeking a way out of inauthentic work, inhospitable relationships, unsustaining professions, and any other sort of dead end. I believe we can, any of us, at any time, pick up a paintbrush and create a new fork in the road to travel that may lead us each to our authentic home, which is deep within, and outward again to our right place in the world.

Part One 🎐 **Beginnings**

Knowing the Imagination

Our imagination is the most important faculty we possess. It can be our greatest resource or our most formidable adversary. It is through our imagination that we discern possibilities and options. Yet imagination is no mere blank slate on which we simply inscribe our will. Rather, imagination is the deepest voice of the soul and can be heard clearly only through cultivation and careful attention. A relationship with our imagination is a relationship with our deepest self. Whether we have cultivated our imagination or not, we each have a lifetime of patterns and habits of thought embedded there, based on past experiences. Our expectations of ourselves and the world flow from these patterns. Suzi Gablik writes: "What we are learning is that for every situation in our lives, there is a thought pattern that both precedes and maintains it. So that our consistent thinking patterns create our experience. By changing our thinking we also change our experience. . . . The basic step is to confront what we actually believe" (p. 27).

Art is a way of knowing what it is we actually believe. Bernie Siegel (1986) is a medical doctor who deeply respects the power of the imagination in regard to physical healing. He asks his cancer patients to draw images of their treatment in order to *discover* their deeply held beliefs about the treatment options. He has learned that the belief of the patient, not the objective benefit of a particular therapy, is the greatest factor determining effective results.

Knowing what our beliefs are requires confronting ourselves, our fears, and our resistance to change. Once we know what our real beliefs are, we can allow them to evolve and change if they do not serve us. Fear will throw up difficult and unpleasant images at the gate of the imagination. Many of us worry that if we delve too deeply, we may find terrible things, or nothing at all, no options, no solutions. Joanna Macy (1983) works with the imagination to get people to break through apathy about being able to affect the ecology of the planet and other big issues facing all of us. She finds that at first fear and despair arise and even seem overwhelming. Once that despair is felt and acknowledged, however, it passes and new options arise that empower individuals to think of new ways to view the problems and to create new solutions.

Art making is a way to explore our imagination and begin to allow it to be more flexible, to learn how to see more options. The major problem for most of us is that we allow fear to stop the imagination before it really begins to work. Shaun McNiff says that the image never comes to harm us, and I agree. Our fears exist to protect us from what we imagine to be harmful. We need to respect their purpose, to see our fears without allowing them to control the great potential of the imagination.

Before trying to change beliefs through making art, begin by taking an inventory of some beliefs that you hold.

Contents of the imagination. Make a list of your beliefs about imagination. Include any phrases or truisms you have heard, like "It's only your imagination," or "You're letting your imagination run away with you." Try to articulate the belief behind such statements. Sort your list into statements of belief that are positive and ones that suggest the imagination is dangerous or trivial. Make a check mark by any of the beliefs you are willing to change. See if you can restate them as beliefs you would like to hold.

The wealth of the imagination. Exercising the imagination is a potent form of preparation for making art. Imagining can be done anywhere, anytime. It is a form of play that feeds our inner self. It is a little like stocking the shelves. Later, at another time, art making can bring forth what we've imagined and allow the image to take form.

The first step is simply to become aware of the endless stream of images that are available during a day. There are visual images, everything from the rumpled bedclothes, your face in the bathroom mirror, and the steam rising from the shower, to the images of suffering children that flash by on the evening news or the pattern of tree branches against the sky that you see as you walk down the street. There are internal images that can be called up at will, like your sister's face when she's laughing, or evoked nonintentionally, as when you remember a special place when you hear a certain song on the radio. Colors, smells, sounds, weather—all of these stimulate imagery to rise within us.

In dreams and daydreams we elaborate images into stories. The imagery of others is also a source; books, movies, poems, are filled with images that we transform by taking them into ourselves. Yet, in order to get through the day, most of the time we screen out images or are only peripherally aware unless something dramatically different comes into view. A spectacular sunset or a car wreck will command our focus on the ride home from work; otherwise we may be lost in thought and oblivious to the images that surround us.

The first step, then, with no outcome in mind, is to begin to practice awareness. Play with the different ways in which you can be aware.

The images are already here. Stop reading for a moment. Sit back in a relaxed posture. Let your eyes fall on the images around you.

Fifteen birds are perched on a wire against a gray November sky outside my window. My desk is crowded with family photos, piles of books, a half-woman, half-deer talisman I made out of sticks, a plastic cow.

Notice the images around you. Appreciate the richness of possibility. Pick one image to follow. Notice its color, shape, texture, detail. Where does it lead you? How did it come to be in front of you? Imagine an art work based on your image. What would it be like? A huge soft sculpture of your stapler? A pencil drawing of the tree outside your window?

Play with your awareness by opening it to include as much as your eyes see. What do you see on the periphery of your vision? Now close your eyes and shift to the pit of your stomach. What is the sensation? What image does it evoke? Open your eyes and go back to your first image. Focus on it; does it seem different? Focus on one detail of that image. Let it go.

Notice what comes up. Sometimes simply shifting our focus to images rather than immersion in our inner dialogue can be a means of achieving relaxation. It is a goalless opportunity for the mind to rest and replenish. At odd moments, practice this skill by choosing to focus on a particular image, then consciously letting it go. It is particularly helpful for relaxation to focus on images of beauty in nature. If your energy is depleted, try focusing on flowers, trees, plants, the sky. Allow yourself to rest in the beauty of what you see, and let that perception replenish your energy. These are very simple means of achieving awareness.

Knowing Memory

When I tried to make sense of how I have used image making as my primary means of making sense of myself and the world, I sifted through memories of my childhood. I was given paint-by-number sets on birthdays and once a paint-on-velvet of a sultry señorita, which I loved for its exotic darkness. The images that hung on the walls at home were few: a calendar in the kitchen from the insurance company, a reproduction of Leonardo's *Last Supper* in the dining room, and in the living room a framed portrait of John F. Kennedy with a lurid tan that had appeared in the Sunday magazine section of the newspaper. There was a statue of Mary on top of the TV and various saints on my bedroom dresser. Art and God were linked visually in my surroundings.

My own early efforts at bringing these two together, however, were not roundly praised. One Sunday, being too ill to attend Mass, I piously constructed my own rosary beads out of materials at hand: orange and yellow beads and a cross fashioned from popsicle sticks, painted purple. I recall looking up from my work past my mother's high heels and beige cashmere coat to her face, aghast at my blasphemy.

At some point I discovered piles of art reproductions in a cupboard: Manet, Van Gogh, Renoir. I never learned where they came from nor their intended purpose. School art consisted of copying a teacher's model drawing, at which I generally succeeded. Once for a high school art assignment we were to copy a famous work of art. I did a dismal rendering of Van Gogh's *Boats on the Beach,* mystified as to why using my tin of watercolors on typing paper yielded such a ghastly, wrinkled failure.

My grandmother took up oil painting a few years before she died. I remember a tiny painting she did of a white dog. But she, like my mother, expended her creative energy in the more traditional arts of cooking, knitting, sewing, and the tatting of lace. None of these skills were passed on to me.

On the day we were to have our kindergarten class photographs taken, I was sent to school in a plain brown dress, a hand-me-down from a cousin, because my mother assumed the picture would be taken in black and white, and she thought a middle tone would show up best. But the picture was in color—something the other mothers must have known, since most of the girls turned up wearing various plaids. Color film was relatively new then, and I still prefer the dreamy black-and-white photos with perforated edges that recorded my earliest life.

In the kindergarten picture I was placed at the end of a row of second-tallest children. I leaned slightly toward the child next to me, afraid I would somehow be cut out of the picture. When I look at this photograph, myself gravely leaning to the right, I see that much of the room and our toys and tables were included in the picture. By age five I thought there might not be room for me within the picture frame, in my brown dress that I did not choose. I thought that life might not have need of me, might crowd me out in favor of others who were brighter, happier, more colorful. My trials, my fears, seemed to me, as I grew up, justly eclipsed by the needs and hardships of others in my life, mostly my mother's.

My parents had four children and not much money. My mother battled cancer throughout most of my childhood and adolescence. My father drank and eventually evolved into an alcoholic. These are terribly bare facts and unfair. Another version would recall my father as a vivid and humorous storyteller and my mother and he creating in our home the gathering place for relatives on holidays full of food and good times. The troubling parts were just facts of life, not questioned or discussed inside the family or out. Yet the emotional part was there, too, and hard to take straight. I detached from it, my father drank and worked two jobs, and I'm still not exactly sure what my brothers and sister did. There's nothing particularly unusual about families not talking about sad and difficult situations.

The power of those images doesn't go away. The feelings leak out in words and actions where they seem out of place. I cried at nearly any provocation during my senior year of high school but never once at my mother's funeral, two years before. Feelings can fester into bitterness, hopelessness, and illnesses of body and soul. My inner life when I was growing up, the subtext below the surface, which looked okay, was a waking nightmare. My mother's illness was its central fact. I sat in algebra class, trying vainly to focus on a problem while my mind wandered over to check the edge of the abyss, wondering, Where is my mother today? Is she at home, taken to the hospital, living, dying, suffering? Her pain took up a great deal of my inner life. I didn't realize it at the time. At the time I was baking cupcakes for a school bake sale and reading J. D. Salinger. Yet inwardly I was also willing my mother to keep living. I breathed her life in and out, trying to keep a tempo, to stay alive, and more important, to keep her alive. It didn't work, of course, and when I was fifteen, she died. I had no idea about grief; what had been put on hold stayed on hold. Now I could live my life, but *who* exactly was "I"? I had spent the greater part of growing up in a prolonged state of emergency. I looked and sounded like a pretty responsible young adult. Inside I was a fluttering bird, an infant crying, a small child hiding behind a door, an embittered, sharp-tongued witch, seething in anger over all she had lost.

Eventually I learned that image making was a way to get at feelings and a means to sort through the facts and fictions of my life. Images have allowed me a return trip, back upstream to where I began, a wondering child sitting in a garden playing as my mother watered flowers and grew tomatoes, before she got sick. Back and back, sitting under a towering maple tree watching clouds of black birds lift off in flight on timeless summer afternoons. Smelling lilies and getting pollen from tiger lillies on my nose, seeking out their scent.

Slowly, in seemingly random order, I traveled back to meet the witch, the child, the creatures of the primordial slime, dragons, snakes, black birds, and black dogs. Paint and chalk and clay have been my tools of alchemy. Image making has been for me the act of taking what was and what never was and creating what is me: a reasonably happy, creative person able to tolerate and embrace the feelings that go along with living, able to connect to others and create meaning.

Our images reveal that we are holographic creatures, living multiple stories. We often get stuck in one view of self and lose the richness of our multiplicity. We get stuck being only a wife, or only a jock, or only a survivor of abuse. Taking one image of self as the sum of who we are is an unnecessary sacrifice. We give up flexibility, spontaneity, and creativity. We manifest our inner conflicts as blockages in our outward life. There are things we do or don't do based on the story of ourselves that we operate from. Yet there are untold other possible stories we might choose from.

The earliest beginnings of our stories are nonverbal images, sights and sounds, smells and gestures of childhood. It is quite possible to go back to one particular image and from it construct an entire story of one's self. There would be an element of truth, but just as a diamond cannot exist with only one facet, the story grown from one image would be quite incomplete. As a diamond has marks and imperfections visible in one facet alongside flawless beauty in another facet of the same stone, so also our images of pain and pleasure exist side by side. No one's life is wholly dark or completely sunny. Images are a means of coming to know the richness and variety of our stories, their shadows and nuances.

Conflicts and contradictions that we encounter in our stories are good places to look deeper. If you were always described as a sunny child, where are the darks that made your brightness so apparent? Perhaps you witnessed these dark elements through a friend or relative rather than experiencing them directly; yet they are still a part of *your* story. If you have memories of great sadness, what were the shafts of light and joy that allowed you relief?

We receive many versions of where we came from and who we

are. Using the image-making process, we can explore our many layers, loosen outworn ideas, and try out new images for ourselves. We enter a world created by others, but we can also create and re-create our world through art making.

Where you come from. Close your eyes and remember your childhood home. What are the images you see? What did your child's eyes and ears store away? Pick a spot in the home and picture yourself there. Jot down a list of the images you see around you. What is the furniture like? What are the colors, the smells, the season, the time of day? How would you describe the image of yourself? Try this at another time in your history, in the same surroundings. Has the image of you changed? Notice the feelings that come up for each image. Just notice and then let them go.

Your art history. What was "art" in your life growing up? Paint-by-number sets? Visits to a museum? Gracious surroundings? Handiwork lovingly made by ancestors? Your sister's activity, but never yours? Classroom crayon drawings posted on the refrigerator? The man who painted landscapes on TV on Saturday afternoons? Write down any memories that come to mind, include attitudes, comments, beliefs, artists you've known or studied or heard about. Notice the place art played in your life. Is it the same now? What is your worst art-related memory? It never fails—when people hear that I am an art therapist, they begin to share an art trauma from grade school, or sometimes much more recently. What is the very best art experience you've ever had?

Finally, let yourself imagine the most pleasurable art fantasy you can. A roommate I had during art school imagined herself traveling to the South of France, meeting Picasso and becoming his model, until he saw her paintings, and then he set down his paintbrush in awe. . . .

Knowing How to Begin

Space

First, clear a space. Walk around your home and look for possibilities. An entire room dedicated to art making is not necessary to begin. A surface is necessary. It can be anywhere you feel comfortable, a basement, a front porch, a corner of the living room. Ask yourself what you need for comfort, how much privacy, how near to others feels right to you. You will eventually make a mess; where can you do this with ease? It is best if you choose a spot that won't need to be dismantled for other uses in between art-making sessions. A dedicated work space, however modest, confirms your intention and allows you to work when you have even brief moments without spending time setting up.

A second important aspect of a work space is a place to display what you do. This can simply mean taping a drawing to a wall near your work surface or it can be placing a drawing board and easel nearby. Keeping your images up and in your visual field is a way to keep the process alive even when you don't have have time to sit down and draw or paint. As you pass by an image, with no real effort, it will begin to speak to you, you will notice things about it. When you actually sit down to work, you will find it easier to know what to do. Much of the process of image work takes place this way, under the surface of everyday life. The image brings to consciousness what you know at deeper levels. You begin to develop a dialogue with your inner self. A dedicated space is a way to welcome your images. If it remains ready for you, even moments while waiting for the laundry to wash or the kettle to boil become fruitful. Think about where you spend time. Sit in different parts of your house. Is the basement cozy? If it feels like a dungeon, go somewhere else. Do you have a room that is rarely used? A friend of mine made a corner of her living room her studio. Think about ease, safety, and comfort. If you build these considerations into your image work space, you will be more likely to use it frequently.

Music

Sound can help create containment in your space. A portable tape or CD player will enhance your work space. Consciously chosen music is preferable to the randomness of radio with its frequent commercial interruptions. Music has a powerful effect and like other aspects of this work requires attention. What sort of music pleases you? I find that instrumental music of all kinds works best for me because with songs I tend to focus strongly on the words and get distracted. Percussion is especially good when focusing on energy awareness in drawing. Unfamiliar music such as chanting, Eastern music that does not rely on familiar Western harmonics, or other world music tapes can open new pathways and spark imagery.

The important thing is to notice whether music helps relax or involve you and increases your enjoyment of the art process. Sometimes just the hum of the refrigerator, birds chirping, or a beating rainstorm is enough.

Begin to notice what pleases you. Experiment and play with sound as an aspect of your space. A source of recordings is suggested in the "Resources" section.

Materials

Before even getting to art materials, ready your space with an empty shoe box without a lid. This is your reference file. A good way to ease into the image process or to participate in it when you have little time, is to feed your reference box. This means simply to collect images that interest you. These can be from any source: magazines, newspapers, photographs, postcards. Collecting images is a way to learn what pleases you. You may use an image as a starting point for your own art work or as a way to learn about the form of an image that interests you, to feed your eyes. These found images can be placed on your display space to instruct you. If you walk by an image of a horse on the wall day after day, you begin to take its form into yourself. When you feel stuck or uninspired, cutting out images is a way to participate in the image process without undue strain. Like weeding a garden, you are cultivating your own images to find out what belongs to you. It is a humble but effective way to begin.

You can also begin to collect small objects the same way. Take another box and drop in items you find on walks: sticks, stones, or any piece of flotsam and jetsam that interests you because of color, shape, or texture. One of my found-object boxes consists entirely of odd bits of rusty metal. I love the many colors of rust, the fact that I usually can't tell what the pieces come from, the odd shapes that smashed bits of metal create. Some are like little landscape fragments, and I have come to think of rust as a metaphor for change, the slow transformation of one substance into another.

Your box can contain absolutely anything and, like the images, becomes a reference file of starting points as well as a cache of materials and a way to get to know your own personal aesthetic.

Art Materials

If your intention is clear to use art as a way of knowing, materials will cooperate in an amazing way to serve you. I have often seen materials behave like the biblical loaves and fishes, somehow being sufficient for the task at hand when to the practical eye they seemed quite inadequate. A lot of fear and resistance gets played out in our attitude toward materials. They can become freighted with intense meaning. I used to have to work up a great sense of entitlement to buy a large box of chalks, only to be paralyzed by their voluptuous abundance. Materials is another area like space where ease and comfort are important. Get what pleases you and enables you to work. If you are a bargain hunter, buy cheap stuff or look for castaways. I know someone who gets all her paper from a billboard company's surplus. The quantities are huge and make her feel very rich, yet the paper is free.

Go to an art supply store and open and touch things. There are always tester samples available. See what you like, and what you can afford. Check out papers. Touch them, feel them, smell them. Disregard what it says on the package. I buy a student grade of watercolor paper and use it for drawing in pastels and painting in acrylics. I like it because its cheap and heavy. If art stores seem intimidating, try a school supply store. Supply catalogues can be a good resource; you can mail-order supplies and have them delivered to your home. Several addresses are listed in the "Resources" section.

The important thing is to notice your *feelings* about supplies. What do you like? What gives you pleasure to use? Specific supplies will be suggested for certain tasks, but in general, to start, a box of twelve or twenty-four soft chalk pastels, a box of sixteen or twenty-four oil pastels, some soft charcoal and soft or medium-soft drawing pencils (2B–5B) are sufficient. Paint can be either tempera, a water-based paint that washes off most surfaces easily, or acrylic, which dries more quickly and can be painted over but must be washed out of brushes right away. Student-grade easel brushes along with inexpensive natural bristle brushes sold in hardware stores in the 1- to 3-inch size are good to have. If you can afford better brushes, that is a good place to spend money because a good brush, well cared for, will last a long time. Collect sponges, rags, and empty containers for water or mixing colors from used kitchen items.

Anything can be turned into a surface on which to paint or draw by applying a coat of gesso or flat white house paint. Gesso is a white acrylic paint that artists use to prepare a canvas for painting. Painting gesso over a piece of cardboard or wood scraps creates a nice surface that accepts paint, pastels, or even pencil. Preparing surfaces with gesso or house paint is another activity that serves the image process in uninspired moments. Having a selection of surfaces gives options and helps you know what feels right as you develop your preferred methods of working.

TIME

Like any other form of practice, art making takes time. The amount of actual doing time can't be prescribed, as it will be different for each person. The image-making time, if only for one or two hours once a week, can be greatly enhanced by the incidental time of just looking at what's been done, just noticing and getting to know the fullness of the image. This looking also serves to motivate. As you look at an image over time, your looking will generate ideas for more images or changes you wish to make will become apparent. Looking is pleasurable and invites you back to create another image.

INTENTION

Clear intention is as important as space and materials. This is the spiritual aspect of art making. Your intention can be simply to have the courage to experiment, or it can be wanting to learn about a problem you are facing. When I enter my art space, I try to have the clearest intention possible to accept whatever comes to me. I trust that the images I need, the knowledge I need, exists within me and that I can access it through this process. If I come in an angry and agitated state, I may ask to be shown the source of these feelings. If I come in confusion, I ask to accept images that will mirror back the components of my confusion. To signal my intention, I sometimes light a candle or a stick of incense before I begin, to mark the time of direct image making. Other times I simply sit in my space or do the chores of cleaning and straightening up to make ready for the time to work. My overall intention is to come to know the source of wisdom and guidance within me. Space and materials are the outward manifestation of my intention.

Part of my intention is to become more aware of my connection to others, and so at times I invite people into my space to work along with me. I find that working in images alongside a friend or loved one is one of the most pleasurable and meaningful ways to spend time together. More about working together with others is included in the section on collaboration in chapter 22.

ATTENTION

Once you feel comfortable with the materials, the process can be used anytime you require guidance, feelings need sorting out, or problems arise. Art making is a way of dwelling in whatever is before us that needs our attention. There is a universal tendency to turn away from difficulty. Image making allows for staying with something while making that staying bearable through the pleasure available in the use of the materials.

It isn't necessary to try to make a picture about the problem; you have only to form a clear intention to know something and then simply take up the materials and begin. Starting with just a mark, continue until the image says it is finished. Usually, I have forgotten the intention while I am immersed in working. When I sit back and look at the image, I recall the intention, and through focusing my attention I get an idea of what, if anything, I need to do next. Sometimes focusing my attention on the image evokes a great deal of feeling. I may have been avoiding some sadness or disappointment; tears may come. That is all part of the process. Feel what comes and let it go. Doubts and judgments will arise. You may at times feel silly or lost. Try simply to notice those feelings and let them pass. The important thing is to begin.

Part Two 🖋 **Basic Steps**

4

Knowing Drawing

Knowing "how to draw," being able to represent objects with a degree of realism, is commonly assumed to be the measure of a true artist. Actually, drawing is energy made visible. Drawing is a way to contact the energy of the subject matter, whether the subject is a still life, a figure, or an inner state of being. The process of drawing is a way to play with and get to know the various forms of energy it is possible to experience.

Before drawing objects outside yourself, it helps to get acquainted with your own energy. You can do this by making marks on paper. Your intention in these initial drawings is to learn about your energy and how it manifests through different materials. Gradually you will get a sense of which material you need for the state you are in at a particular time. For now, just getting to know the possibilities is enough.

This is a point where music is helpful. I like to play percussion tapes, but you may find that other types of music are helpful. Experiment with your own favorites, and try a few of the tapes from the catalogue recommended in the "Resources" section.

Choose any size paper and either pencil or charcoal to begin. Make marks, lines, shapes on the paper without representing any object. Fill the paper as completely as you can. Step back when you are done. Notice your energy as it appears on the page. Is it dense, airy, flowing, nervous, playful? Choose another sheet, either larger or smaller, and with a different medium, do another page of marks. If you began by sitting, stand for your second drawing. How was your energy affected by the changes you made? Do you have a different result standing than sitting? Which feels better to you? Try a very tiny drawing, two inches by two inches. Try a very large drawing. Explore different ways to make marks: exert pressure or lighten up. Smear charcoal with your fingers and rub it in to make a gray ground, then draw on top of the gray field with strong black strokes.

Make as many drawings as you need to find a size and shape of paper and a type of line and pressure that feels pleasurable to you today. There is no right or wrong here, simply the exploration of possibility. Big, loose drawings are not better than small, contained ones. Precise isn't more precious than loopy or meandering.

When you have about ten drawings, whether it takes one hour or several days, spread them out on your display space and notice the different ways your energy manifests. If you are journaling along with your image process, see if words come to describe your drawings. If not, just look and appreciate your work. Notice if you have a physical reaction to any of the drawings. Where does your eye go naturally? Is one set of marks relaxing as your eye follows its pattern? Is another energizing? You are building a vocabulary of marks that can both reflect and create energy states. If you let your first drawing of any session be automatic, just choosing a material and letting your body speak, you can see what kind of energy you have at that moment. By choosing to deliberately make certain kinds of marks, you can change your energy and feeling state.

When I am anxious, I tend to draw circles and fill them in with shades from dark to light; this soothes me. Drawing very large and loose opens me up. Using my whole body, drawing from my feet up through my shoulders and arm and hand, brings energy up and outward, leaving me feeling more alive. I have boxes of old business cards, the backs of which are the perfect size for tiny drawings on days when too much is happening and I feel overwhelmed.

Experiment with different kinds of drawings, with your only goal being to see what feels right to you. Is a tiny sheet of paper cozy or claustrophobic? Is a large sheet overwhelming or exhilarating? Does white space left on the page feel restful or empty?

Notice any thoughts that arise as you draw. You may find you

have rules about drawing embedded within you that you didn't realize. This sort of mark making sometimes evokes old memories of
being told not to scribble, that "scribble-scrabble" is for babies, isn't
drawing, is a waste of time. This, of course, is not true. If you go to
a museum or look in books of art of the old masters, you will see
that every drawing, no matter how precisely realistic, is built up of
areas of marks—areas of scribble, in fact. Taking away these energetic
marks would rob a drawing of its vital force and power.

Was drawing first presented to you as a task of filling in the lines
drawn by someone else? When I was in kindergarten, coloring outside the lines was considered a mistake and meant forfeiting the
chance to draw. Sometimes having a structure to fill in can be soothing: knowing where the boundaries are is reassuring. If that is your
only experience of drawing, however, you learn only to adjust your
energy to fit the spaces allotted to you by others, and never find out
how to manage and enjoy the natural flow of your own energy in
the world. While this intention is not stated out loud, it is conveyed
in the task and is taken into consciousness by doing the task.

Once you begin to shift your perception to drawing-as-energy,
notice how your concept of "drawing" can expand. The patterns of
footprints in the schoolyard snow are a drawing made by exuberant
children at recess. Trees draw spidery shadow lines across the sunlit
floor. Cracks in the sidewalk sketch a torso. Drawing is energy made
visible.

DRAWING OBJECTS

Drawing an object is a way to get acquainted with and connected to
the energy of that object in a powerful way. I choose to draw objects
that I love or ones that have something to teach me. Drawing things
is a kind of lovemaking, so the subject should be chosen carefully. I
like to draw spiky artichokes and voluptuous, curving peppers.
Drawing is a way of knowing the essence of things—"seeing infinitude in the ordinary," a friend of mine says. Working in this way
forms a relationship to the energy of the subject. Drawing can be a
celebration of the ponderous energy of a granite mountain or the

simple curving line of a tree that puts you back in touch with the miracle of the seasons.

Choose a subject that pleases you. To begin, choose something small enough to handle and be left on your drawing table. Allow it to enter your awareness visually as completely as you can. Travel lovingly over the contours of your subject. Discover your intention in relation to this object. Is it to know about the dark hollow of a cut melon or the gnarled complexity of a tree root? Ask your subject to teach you about itself. As you move your eye along the contours of your subject, move your hand on the paper, recording what you see.

Keep your effort simple, to learn the essential shapes. Draw only as long as you feel connected. If you begin to struggle, stop, let it go. Go back to just looking. As soon as you feel connected once more to the beauty of the object, resume drawing. Or, if this doesn't work, try again later. Drawing is a relationship and can't be forced. The primary obstacle to drawing is losing focus on the subject and shifting consciousness to judging the resulting drawing, which is only a record of the energy between you and your subject. Even a record of a struggle is a useful drawing and affords lots of learning.

If you discover that you really like drawing objects, consider getting a sketchbook and drawing the same object until every page is filled. Choose something simple and let yourself see it as deeply as you can. Drawing in this way is a meditation. It is especially helpful as a balance to drawings focused on your inner process. If you decide on this course of drawing the same object, choose playfully. What do you really want to know more about? Choose things to draw that you want to have in your life. If you wish to be a writer, draw your cup of pens and writing tools. If you wish to be more grounded and steady, draw a mountain; more orderly, the pattern of a brick wall or a well-made fence.

This is neither silliness nor magic but rather a way to state your intention and take action to clarify it. Without action, however small, our intentions cannot manifest but remain wishful thinking. As you draw your chosen object say, a clock if you have trouble with time—you are dwelling in that issue. The act of drawing represents a commitment to focus on something. Surprising insights arise as you turn your attention to the object through drawing.

There are whole books written about drawing real things. If this kind of image making has captured you, you may wish to consult several title listed in the "Suggested Reading" section of the bibliography (see Edwards, Franck, and Nicolaides listings). Remember that reading about drawing, however interesting, is never as good as drawing itself.

DRAWING IN COLOR

Chalk pastels make an easy transition from charcoal, having a similar consistency. Open your box and let a color choose you. Color is feeling made visible. Begin again by filling a page with marks using just this one color. Besides the kinetic energy of mark making, you now have the emotional energy of color to play with. Using color is another source of deepening our knowledge of self and the world. Choose one or two more pastels to go with your first color and start a new drawing. Let the colors mingle and smear. Use the chalk on its edge and then on its side. Use your fingers to blend the colors into new shades. When you feel you are done, take a new sheet of paper, perhaps larger than before. Choose three more colors, ones that do not seem compatible with one another or ones that you don't particularly like. Notice what it is like to use these colors.

Do at least one drawing using all the colors. Do one more using only the colors you like best. Hang up all your work. Sit and look. Look until your eye decides which drawing you prefer and see if you can say why. Does this piece evoke a particular feeling: tranquillity, anger, sadness, joy? Or an emotional tone: subdued, somber, rollicking, confused? Just sit with your work; these are maps of yourself. If you are journaling, write a stream-of-consciousness response to your colors. Allow whatever comes up to be welcome: memories, dreams, fragments of dialogue or story. To gain what your drawings have to give, you must witness them. Treat them like friends. You wouldn't run around and ignore a friend who came to visit—you would sit down and pay attention, making the person feel welcome.

Next time, start by using your favorite color or color combination. Make a mark and let it call forth the next mark, inviting the colors to mingle as they choose. You are beginning to develop your own palette, learning which colors nourish you. At the end of a recent workshop, during the sitting-and-looking time, someone noticed that each of us was wearing the colors that showed up in our work. Notice the colors in your surroundings. Do you make a conscious effort to choose the colors you wear or those in your home? Are you living in your preferred palette? Begin to notice colors as you go about your day, in restaurants and doctor's offices, in the homes of friends. Where do you feel most alive, most yourself? What colors are present in those environments?

OIL PASTELS

Oil pastels introduce the element of resistance. They require a little more effort than chalks and charcoal. The colors are vivid and the oil binder makes them slippery and greasy rather than dusty like chalks. Start with a smaller piece of paper, 8 by 12 inches or less. See if the same colors speak to you in this medium. Let one color begin the drawing and call forth the next. Layer the colors, letting mark blend into mark. Experiment with smudging the colors and leaving areas of pure color. Try scratching into the surface after you have built up several layers.

You may enjoy using oil pastels in a painterly fashion. Turpenoid can be used to loosen the oil and allow the color to flow more freely. Turpenoid is a synthetic form of turpentine, without the dangerous fumes. It is, however, flammable, and while it is not dangerous to breathe, it is toxic if swallowed and should be used carefully around children and pets, who may mistake it for water. Put a small quantity in a glass jar labeled prominently and clean up carefully when finished. A heavier surface is better if you choose to use Turpenoid with oil pastels. Gesso-coated cardboard or wood scraps or bristol board, a heavier type of drawing paper, all work well. You can dip the oil pastel into the turpenoid, or you can brush it over the drawing to achieve a wash. If this method appeals to you, you may want to move on to painting, which uses color even more directly. Notice your reaction to this material in its many forms. Some people hate oil pastel and find it smelly, dirty, and imprecise. To others it is sensuous, creamy, and rich. What is important is coming to know what feels good to you.

You have now experimented with several types of drawing materials and surfaces which can be used in endless combinations. A heavy pencil over an oil pastel drawing will etch the surface in an interesting way to add definition. A thin wash of Turpenoid and oil pastel provides a colored ground for a charcoal drawing. When you are working with washes, veils of color leads into painting, which is introduced more fully in the next chapter.

5

Knowing Painting

Painting is allowing feelings to become visible through color, color applied in sensuous strokes, with a brush or even with your fingers. Paint is feeling liquified. Feeling connotes a relaxation of reason, and painting lets us put reason aside momentarily and enter a different realm. While it is possible to paint realistically, that is not our present goal. Our intention is to use paint to explore the realm of feeling and emotion through color. Because paint is a fluid medium, it evokes a particularly sensuous energy.

Tape the corners of a large piece of paper, at least 18 by 24 inches, to your work surface. Choose a large brush, 2 inches wide or so. Have a container of clean water nearby and a sponge or rag to blot excess water from your brush. See which color is asking to be used. Put some of this color on your palette. When using acrylic paints, I use a piece of glass, 12 by 14 inches with a piece of white paper taped to the underside, fastened around each edge with masking tape. The colors stand out against the white surface, and the palette cleans up easily with a straight-edge razor knife. You can also use an old dinner plate, but it is a bit harder to clean. If you decide on tempera paints, an old muffin tin works better than glass, since tempera is more fluid than acrylic paint.

Begin with one color and, while standing, cover your paper with it. This is your ground of feeling. Notice your body as you apply the paint. Where does the movement of painting originate? In your hand, arm, shoulder, torso? Can you feel your legs and feet as you paint? How does it feel to daub color, to make broad sweeping strokes? Make the process of applying color as pleasurable as you can.

Like paint, emotions are the "colors" of experience; without them life is wooden and dull. Emotion is a physical experience. When we are physically unaware, we have limited access to our emotions. Paying attention to how our body feels and adjusting our movements to create the most enjoyable sensation helps to increase our access. We shut off access to our emotions because of experiences of fear in our lives. By gently listening to our bodily cues and responding to them with small adjustments, we create trust in ourselves. While you are painting, if you begin to feel anxious, just stop for a moment and remind yourself that you are safe, that your intention is to explore emotions at the best pace for you. Resolve that you will listen carefully and create a trusting partnership between your self and your emotions.

You have covered your paper in pure color, yet feelings are rarely unadulterated. More often feelings are complex, mixed, muted, even at times kaleidoscopic, changing even as we try to name them. Choose a second color. Experiment with your options, paint over areas, and let the two colors mix and mingle, obliterate one another, and create entirely new colors. Play with the paint on the page. Is one color stronger, more easily overcome? Do the colors blend harmoniously or clash? Notice your response to the colors as they change. Do you miss the simplicity of the pure color, or do you like the swirling mixture? Does the page seem muddy or mysterious, defiled or delightful? When you feel finished, put your painting aside. Rinse your brushes and change your painting water.

For your next piece, begin with a dark color. Create your ground by covering the entire paper. See if you can find a rhythm in putting down the color, slow down your strokes, lighten your touch. Exper iment with having the brush so full of paint that it drips. Choose a second color; make it a light one. Be sure to have clean water and a clean brush. What happens when you try to add light to dark? Is the delicate shade swallowed by the dark ground, or do traces remain?

For your next painting, tape a heavy piece of paper to a drawing board. The drawing board can be a piece of masonite, wood, or any other rigid surface that you can pick up and move around. Tape all the edges firmly with masking tape. The paper will buckle when wet, and the tape will help it to dry more or less flat.

Take your largest brush and paint the surface of your paper with clear water. Using any colors that please you, drop paint onto the wet ground and notice how it behaves. Tilt the board and allow color to run and make shapes. Resist any effort to make the shapes into something recognizable. Simply practice putting reason aside and letting the paint create the painting. Add more water if necessary with a spray bottle or brush. Experiment with more and less watery paint to create darker and lighter veils of color. Play with the possibilities. When you feel finished, put this painting aside, but leave it taped to the board until it dries thoroughly.

Choose three colors that feel compatible to you for the palette of your next piece. Focus on your movement with no other goal in mind than the dance of color and shape on the page. Cover the surface, letting the colors play and blend together. See how many variations result from the interplay of the three colors. See how pleasurable you can make the resulting colors to your eye. Notice once again where in your body you are painting from. What parts of you are involved? Are there any parts that feel absent?

Do at least one more painting, using any of the methods you have tried or a new one that you invent. When you have five or so paintings, gather them together and sit with them and look. What do you see? Where is your eye drawn? Do the paintings seem like images of feelings to you? Reflect on the physical act of painting.- What part of you seemed to be in charge? How is painting different from drawing for you? What did you find most pleasurable in painting?

The pleasure we take in making images is important because pleasure opens us. If you can allow yourself experiences of pleasure in painting, you will become more open to knowing and feeling in a deep way. This is our intention when painting, to experience pleasure and increase knowledge of emotions. It is our emotions that move us to take action. By fully exploring and knowing our emotions, we are more likely to take right action from a clear place

For your next session of painting, think of an experience in which you felt strong emotion or one where you emotions were unclear. Once you have chosen an experience to paint from, close your eyes and sit with it for a few moments. Ask yourself, what color is the ground of this experience? Take the first answer that comes. Resist second-guessing; so what if you hear pink and it is an experience of anger? If you get no answer, open your eyes and choose a color as quickly as you can without thinking. In either case, trust and begin to paint. Once you have put down the ground, ask what color comes next. If shapes or images emerge, accept them, but don't make a conscious effort to represent ideas about the situation. You already know what your ideas are; now you want additional knowledge that is within you but not so readily available.

It is fine to forget all about what you are trying to learn and just let the painting paint itself. When you come to a stopping point, step back and see if your eye is satisfied. Are you stopping because you are done or because you are reluctant to go on? Look to your body for the answer. Are you feeling relaxed and grounded, or is your breathing shallow and anxious? You are free to stop in any case, of course, but it is good to begin to know why you do certain things and to accept your reasons. If you are stopping because of any fear or reluctance about going on, wash out your brushes and clean up your area a bit before you sit down to look at your work. Cleaning up is an important aspect of image making. It provides a transition from the deep involvement and restores a sense of equilibrium and safety.

When you sit down to contemplate your painting, recall the situation you began with and hold it in mind while you look but without coming to conclusions. What is the painting showing you? What does it mirror back? Have your feelings shifted or become clearer? Take in what your can. Journal your reactions if you wish. Sometimes a painting speaks with undeniable clarity right away; more often, the message gets absorbed slowly over time. Let the painting stay on your wall for a while, and it will yield its wisdom as you can receive it.

Color

Knowing color is a source of deepening our understanding of self and the world. Our individual responses to color are the best place to begin. Reflect on your paintings and see if you can discern for yourself what feelings are evoked by the colors you used. You needn't understand why a color means a certain thing, simply that it does mean that for you right now. Later, if you want, you can investigate the universal meanings of color, which can enrich your appreciation of the interconnectedness of all beings. In general, every color contains a paradox of opposite meanings. Red can connote rage and violence with images of carnage and bloody death but also the pulsing blood of new life and the passion of love. Green is putrid, festering gangrene as well as delicate spring leaves. Fertile earth is black, as are the charred remains of a burnt-out building. Our ethnic and religious background contributes to the emotional meaning of color, as do the places where we have lived, which give us an inborn affinity for certain shapes, colors, and space configurations. The physical and emotional are intertwined deeply within us. We shake with rage and see red, cringe in fear and are yellow with cowardice, are in the pink and dance with joy. Through painting we come to see and appreciate both the uniqueness and the richness of our moving and feeling self.

6

Knowing Sculpture

Sculpture is the process of giving three-dimensional form to our experience. The root of the word *sculpture* means "to carve," and for many people the carved marble statues of classical antiquity or Michelangelo leap to mind as an image. By slightly shifting perception, it is possible to look at ordinary objects, indeed everything around us, as sculpture. Take a moment and scan your immediate environment. Relax and let the familiar labels of the objects surrounding you fall away. Instead of desk, couch, light fixture, stove, or bicycle, see sculptural form, see cylinder, rectangle, sweeping curve, angular box.

Sculpture need not be carved; it can also be assembled by adding together pleasing shapes. It can even be discovered. You have discovered sculpture if you have ever picked up a piece of driftwood or an oddly shaped stone. Something in your inner experience resonated with what you picked up with that particular stone. Perhaps it resembled a human figure, or you saw an animal in a piece of wood. Images that are necessary to us come in all sorts of ways, for the soul never tires of trying to make itself known. Sometimes in the image process we begin with experience and try to express it. Working in assemblage, the art of putting things together to form a new expression, we begin with an object and through our resonance discover our experience and its meaning.

If you have a found-object box in your art space, look through it and choose or be chosen by several objects. Try not to think too hard about your choices. If you don't yet have a collection, take a walk in nature or visit a junkyard or thrift store. Choose objects that delight or intrigue, confuse or repel you. Play with grouping them in pleasing arrangements. Make a space for your objects, and over the course of the next week, arrange and rearrange them as the spirit moves you. Notice if your assemblage is asking for more color or more shapes. Does it want something vertical? Something round? Try to lose the names of the objects. Look at your arrangement in different lights: in the morning and before you go to bed with the lights low. Look at it from above and crouch down to eye level. Can anything be taken away? Do you like simple, spare assemblage or rich piles of multiple shapes? Are all your objects from nature, or do you mix in manufactured ones as well? Notice what your eye likes. This attention acquaints you with your own sense of beauty, your own aesthetic.

After you have lived with the movable arrangement of objects for a while, decide to commit yourself to an assemblage. Figure out the best way of joining your objects. Should they be bound together with string? Nailed? Glued? Experiment with different adhesives. Wood glue, a yellow, stronger version of white glue, works well for most natural items. Hot glue guns are quick and effective but won't adhere slick surfaces like plastic or metal. Notice carefully the experience of committing to each piece.

Sit with your piece and look at it from all angles. What does it feel like all together? Does it seem finished, does it need a box, a pedestal, a light shining down on it? "Finishing" is a momentary experience, and the chance to change or take apart or add to your piece always remains. An assemblage can be very much like a dream, with fragments of many incongruous items that add up to convey a meaning or a story that can scarcely be put into words.

Following from assemblage is found-object sculpture, where objects are altered more purposefully to create a particular image. I had a piece of tree root in my studio for months that evoked a flying figure to me, but was headless. This stage in the process is like the play of small children, for whom a tiny scrap can be invested with great meaning. Then one day on a walk, I found the head—a small piece of weathered wood that resembled a bird's head to me. I joined the two pieces with plastic wood after whittling off bits of wood to

Fig. 1. Shaman's Drum *(painted wood, mixed media).*

clarify the image of the bird-headed figure that I saw in the object. Slowly the figure emerged but then sat for almost a year until I figured out how to make it seem like it was flying. I just looked at it day after day until it became clear that I could drill a hole and insert a stick, anchored in a wad of wood dough, a product available in hardware stores and used for filling in cracks in wooden furniture or trim. Embellished with feathers and a drum made from a film container lid, wire and beads, Shaman's Drum eventually came to be (fig. 1).

This piece, which evolved over several years, was worked on mostly indirectly. Each time, I went as far as the "don't know" place and stopped. Patient waiting is sometimes a big part of image making, just resting in not knowing and trusting that eventually, if I maintain my connection to a piece and don't abandon it, resolution will eventually come.

Clay is a good medium for coming to know visceral experience. Strong, instinctual experiences lend themselves to expression in this simple material, which requires no tools but can be shaped directly with the pressure of your hands. If you wish to contact your gut, clay, which is slippery and dark and evokes dirt or even excrement, provides swift passage.

Throw an old plastic tablecloth or shower curtain or a heavy piece of canvas over your work table, and simply shake it out and roll it up when you finish clay work. There is no need to wash it; just store it for future use. Clay can be obtained from pottery supply outlets, and for your purpose here, the least costly will do very well. Kept it in a tightly sealed plastic bag, clay will remain workable indefinitely. If it gets too stiff, add a wet sponge to the bag, and the clay will reabsorb moisture as needed.

Tear off a good-sized fistful of clay. Sit with it, holding, tearing, kneading it, noticing your response. Do any words leap to mind? Slimy, slippery, dirty, sensuous, pliable, soft, creamy? Pay attention to your breathing and to your gut. What comes up? Let memories, feelings, or thoughts rise and fall in your mind as you handle the clay. Close your eyes. Move your awareness to your hands, then to your shoulders, your lower pelvis. Try touching the clay very lightly, then more strongly. Notice what feels best to you, most effortless. Continue that movement, that form of touch. See how you can adjust your method to find what is best for you. How does it feel to stand and squash the clay with your feet? To squeeze it through your fingers? To roll it out and pound it flat?

Does an image want to be made? If so, follow it, trying to stay focused on your breathing. If the image changes and transforms as you work, let it go and become something else. The changeable nature of clay is a wonderful reflection of mind and the endless coming and going of images. Do any voices pipe up saying "Don't make a mess," "Don't get dirty," "Don't play with mud"? If so, ask, "Why not?" See what sort of answer you get. Is it satisfactory? If it feels right to you, consider adding a small amount of water to your clay and actually making mud. You can do this in an old baking pan or dish pan. What is the experience of mud for you? When you feel finished, let the clay settle in its container. Pour off any clear water, but be sure not to pour clay down any pipes where it can settle and cause a blockage. Journal about this experience if memories or feelings arise.

If in your clay work you do end up with an image that you wish to keep, simply let it dry. Even without kiln firing, clay pieces will last indefinitely. When dry, they can be painted with acrylic paint or coated with a mixture of one part white glue and one part water to provide a protective skin. I have had several unfired clay pieces for over fifteen years with no deterioration. Yet clay is endlessly recyclable. If you wish to reuse it at any point, break up dry clay and soak it in water. Let the water evaporate until the clay is malleable, and use it again.

If you have created an image that expresses a painful or traumatic experience, consider placing the finished piece outside in the elements, where you can watch it return to the earth, taking your pain along with it. Over time, rain and wind will slowly wear away the image until it's gone. Try to have a clear intention to let go of the pain associated with the experience. See if you can imagine it seeping back into the earth to be reabsorbed and released. This meditation is valuable in making the return of all things more understandable.

Reflect on your clay experience. Is clay primarily a kinesthetic experience of touch and movement for you? Did the clay serve to relax you by receiving your excess energy, or did your viscera get stirred up? Does clay loosen old memories, feelings, or dreams? Clay, like all art materials, serves many purposes. As you become acquainted with it, you will discover your most congenial relationship—or maybe that you'd rather not have a relationship at all! Just knowing clay's basic properties helps you to have another option and avenue when certain images arise. I don't use clay very often, but in chapters 12 and 16 I tell of two instances when clay was absolutely necessary and I was glad to have had a bagful stashed away to use.

The final form of sculpture presented here uses simple kitchen materials: masking tape and aluminum foil. I learned this method from my friend, an artist and art therapist, Don Seiden, who has made both small-scale pieces and a life-size sculpture adapting tape and foil. This method is especially effective for creating figures, binding together the elements, which are twisted and shaped out of foil, with the tape. The foil can be the cheapest generic brand, but the tape should be of good quality or else it will not hold together. The figures created are somewhat bendable. Once you have positioned your piece to your liking, use acrylic paint to bring it alive. Fabric and other materials can be used for embellishment, but painting alone can be enough.

Begin with a simple human figure or animal, and allow its personality to evolve as you create. You may want to create an environment or a companion for your creation. These sculptures lend themselves to narratives. See if a story emerges as you mold your figures. We all have a cast of internal characters. Sculpting them is one way to get to know them, to honor them and respect them. Who lives in you whom you might like to know better, to play with or learn from?

It takes a while to make these images. Any process that takes time but doesn't require too much thinking allows you to dwell in the image longer and absorb more of the nuances of meaning. These figures can be totems embodying a quality you want to develop or understand. State your intention to your figure and ask what it needs to help you—maybe an environment, maybe a shrine. Explore the story and myth of your figure—playful-like-a-rabbit, strong-like-a-bull—and let it emerge over time.

In my work, characters that first emerged independently eventually wound up in a scene together, which I call a story box (fig. 2). The dog and devil were each done for different demonstrations, but after a while they asked for a sleeping man and later an angel. After several years, my story box *Night of the Soul* was finished, housed in an old grocery carton, cut and painted. All the figures are of foil and

Fig. 2. Story Box: Night of the Soul *(mixed media).*

tape, though embellished with a few found objects. The fire is painted foil with no tape.

Don't be concerned if you tape up a figure rather quickly and it sits and sits, refusing to be painted or to divulge its story. Trust that a process is taking place, even if it isn't conscious. Pay attention to the piece, handle it once in a while, and recall your intention. Notice whether you are avoiding the figure's completion, and let the figure know you welcome it when it is ready to arrive. Write down any stories that develop.

A variation on this method uses plaster gauze to cover the taped foil armature. Plaster gauze is available in rolls from art and school supply stores. Cut the gauze into strips and dip it in water. Then wrap it around your piece, smoothing as you go. The plaster will harden into a very durable sculpture that has a nice surface for painting. Additional features of a figure can be built up using the plaster gauze.

You are now acquainted with a wealth of methods with which you can welcome your images. Some can be used as a warm-up anytime, not only for art making but to get your energy flowing for any type of creative work. The simple, nonobjective painting, drawing, and clay serve as relaxation and centering tools. The found-object assemblage and sculpture provide a starting point for exploration. All of these methods can be the basis for knowing any sort of life experience, emotional or otherwise, that arises. By experimenting and learning what particular materials and tasks are most pleasureable to you, many new options exist for the soul to manifest its wisdom in your life. In subsequent chapters you will learn in greater detail how to go deeper with images and to understand and use the twin concepts of intention and attention.

Part Three *Personal Content*

7

Knowing Obstacles

Morning sunlight streams through the windows of the library in an aging mansion that now houses the art department of a small women's college in New England. Mr. Marcus, the instructor, pokes me sharply between the shoulders with his cane. "Stop thinking and paint!" he bellows. The model sits before me, an ordinary-looking woman with long brown hair and gray eyes. She wears an orange sweater and jeans. I stare at the model and try to let my hand follow the contours of her face. I walk a tightrope when I paint. Not thinking terrifies me. The answer is to look. The more I look, the more I see. I get lost in the shadow under her left eye; I see purple, green, gray. I forget to think. I paint. Suddenly people are moving around, the three-hour class is over, it's lunchtime. Mr. Marcus nods at me.

I am outside myself when I paint. No, I am outside my head when I paint. For what seems like the first time in my life, I step out of the watchtower that is my usual consciousness. And no disaster takes place. Another part of me is at work here, a part I am unfamiliar with, if I know it at all.

Painting, I discover, can extinguish my usual mode of being, thinking, analyzing, judging. Actually, until I began to paint, I never realized how completely those activities consume me, how little I really look at the world around me. I paint a lot. I copy paintings of great artists. Some of the other teachers jokingly call this "Mr. Marcus's forgery class," but when I copy an obscure Picasso painting of a cherry tomato plant growing out of a can, I put down paint in ways I don't know how to. These strokes are fresh and free, as if I am dancing with Picasso and letting him lead. It feels safe, the way tracing a picture is to a fearful child.

Mostly I paint portraits. I ask Bill, the night guard in the art buildings, to pose for me. He sits at a desk in the foyer every night as students come and go working on projects. He tells corny jokes and reminds me a little bit of my father; he has a lived-in face. On the evening we arrange, I show up with my paint and a newly stretched canvas. Bill has on a shirt and tie, his sparse, gray hair slicked down over the bald spot. He holds himself stiffly, not smiling. I finish the portrait in one sitting. I don't pay too much attention to Bill's torso; his burgundy dress shirt and plaid tie are filled in without much detail or nuance. I concentrate on the face. Bill looks much more formal and severe than usual, but I can't change that. If I try to decide the sort of effect I want, something rebels and the painting doesn't work. I can't lie in a painting; I don't have that skill. Something paints that is not my usual mind. Once the image is down, I can't suspend judgment, can't not think. So I paint holding my breath, fearful of losing my ephemeral passport into the process. I don't compose, I don't do backgrounds, I can't afford to. I choose people who interest me, who have a face I like or an energy that attracts me. I pick someone who is at home in his face. I don't know this at the time.

But I do know that when Pat Geohagen, my ceramics teacher, comes to sit, she had curled her hair, put on mascara and a stylish sweater. I don't know what to do. I love her for the dirt under her fingernails, the clay-smeared pants and torn shirt, her hair tied carelessly under a bandanna, bags under her eyes from a long night of coffee, cigarettes, and firing the big gas kiln. But she's my teacher and she honors me, not just by coming to sit but by presenting her "best" face. I just smile and start to paint. The portrait shows her a little stilted, her face composed as if for a photograph. Like Bill, sitting for a portrait is a big thing for Pat. Of course it is, but I'm not thinking about that. Best faces are not what I need to learn about, not what I am hungry for. My own best face is like a porcelain mask. Not that I'm carefully made up. To everyone I'm sure it's quite an ordinary face. But the face I hold up in public strives for perfection.

It's killing me. It isn't really a face I need to paint, it's a soul. Truth, not artifice, not persona. I have plenty of that.

I end up frustrated with Pat's portrait, but she likes it, or says she does, and I am happy to give it to her. I'm stuck. I have no words for the problem. There is something I need from painting people, but I don't know what it's called or how to ask for it, and my sitters, by dressing up, are not giving it to me. Then it occurs to me—Chris Osage. I admire Chris, an art history major who takes some art courses. She's older than me, tall, cadaverously thin, a face full of menace. It's a quiet menace, no bravado. She says what she wants and doesn't give a damn what anyone else thinks. Chris agrees to sit for a portrait as long as she doesn't have to get dressed up. She shows up wearing a ratty green sweater with cigarette burns in it and dirty jeans. No makeup, her hair isn't even combed. She sprawls across the ugliest chair in the room, a brown plastic armchair, and fixes me with her habitual scowl. This can't be a one-shot job, I realize. I can't get everything I need in one sitting. The canvas is four by four feet, and her body is important, it says as much as her face; I want to get the gesture of the figure as well as the expression of the face. I tell Chris I need more time, and we plan to meet again in a couple of days. I sit back and look at the portrait. What I have so far is strong and true, a real face. A woman's face, uncomposed, not striving for beauty, full of storms of emotion that well up from an inner place. But the body . . . For the first time I see the body as active and expressive, the source and conduit of the feelings I read upon the face. I can draw the body. My life drawings are successful because I can see the human form as an object, a collection of beautiful shapes and lines. But I don't draw the face of the life model. Life drawing is about the abstract beauty of the human form, not about personality. I want to get it all in a painting at the same time, but I don't know how. Painting is a way of knowing. If I keep painting, maybe I will get to know what an honest face is for myself. Maybe I'll get to live in my body.

The problem is, the minute I sit down again before a partially finished canvas, the voices start. Damning, critical voices, full of derision for my efforts, voices attached to eyes that see only flaws. They prevent the process of immersion, they flay and destroy me. The arm is too long, the left eye wanders . . . something is wrong. The problem is, once I look at a fragment of the painting and try to rework it, I kill it; the arm becomes severed emotionally from the rest of the figure. I am enfeebled by the chorus of voices that moves quickly to a taunting chant: Why are you doing this? Where will this get you? You need a job, art is not a job, you aren't entitled to this. Why paint? You have no idea what you are doing. Until finally I drop my brush and flee. These are my usual voices, my inner dialogue, honed from years of critical thinking, looking for flaws as a means of staying safe. Painting must be very dangerous because it calls these voices out in magnum force.

I am on my way to meet Chris for our second sitting when my eye falls on a half bottle of rotgut wine on the windowsill, left over from the weekend. It's cheap and warm, but one glass might help me relax. I pour a half glass and drink it down and take the bottle with me. All I have to finish is the lower part of Chris's body and that ugly chair. I'm not going to mess with the face or hands. Chris has some wine too, and lets her cigarette burn down in the metal ashtray. Halfway through my third glass I notice that I am painting and the voices are fainter, scratchy and far away like an old record being played in another room. Triumph. I declare the painting finished that night and go back to my room to sleep it off.

I wake up the next day, crabby with a pounding headache and dry mouth. The painting of Chris is chosen for a student show. For a month it stares menacingly down over the wooden bannister of the grand staircase up to the second floor of the art building. My teachers tell me it is very good. They don't understand when it is the last portrait I paint that semester. I grew up with a father who was full of alcohol's illusory courage. I heard him talk about his dreams and watched him end up with only shadows. I'll be damned if I will drink to paint. There has to be another way. I have no idea what that way might be. I am furious that the wine even helped, that the portrait turned out well. I know a bad bargain when I see one.

Still, I touch something in painting that feels alive and real, like stepping into a cold river and being shocked awake. I want to know how to get to that place. Drinking gets me the illusion of that place. You can be standing in warm pee and believe you're in the cold river with a few drinks. I know if I had started the portrait of Chris drinking, it probably wouldn't have turned out. Critical thinking banishes the state of flow, and the thing about drinking is, when it wears off, it turns up the volume of that critical voice. In an instant I am standing in a cracked, dry river bed, vultures circling overhead.

Painting wakes me up, the smell of oil and turpentine, the voluptuous smearing of paint onto a pliant, resilient surface. For a while after painting, my vision remains vivid. I notice the grain in the wood of the paneled walls, the polished surface of the bannister under my hand as I descend the staircase, feel the weight of the wrought-iron gate as I let myself out into the day, which, for a while at least, I see with a clarity that is almost painful, that is joy. I want this in my life, and I know that alcohol is a false payment. What the real price of clarity is, I have no idea, but I am convinced that I will pay it.

Although I couldn't name it for many years, in painting I encountered the power of the inner critic to control and limit my life. This force that counters the desire to create is within each of us. Generally the critic doesn't appear in full force until you are in a situation where you have the opportunity to do what you want, something important and self-chosen, something with risk. For me this happened in college when I could choose my own course of study. Before then, the critic maintained a certain level of toxic chatter in response to daily life. Art making increased the volume. At first, when I dared to choose art, there was a thrilling sense of freedom, but fairly quickly, resistance arose.

Perhaps your inner critic appeared while you were trying the methods in the earlier chapters. Perhaps, like me when I painted Chris, you felt a certain resistance to going on. Did you find yourself discovering more important things than art making? Laundry or errands can suddenly take on great value. Did eating or drinking or using other substances get in your way? How about suddenly finding the needs of others more pressing than the need to draw or paint? If you found that you inexplicably lost interest or just weren't getting to your art time, after initially enjoying it, your inner critic was arising. For some people, the critic is very active already. You've seen and heard its power when you've resolved to write or perform or sculpt and then didn't stay with it.

The inner critic in some form is universal and has nothing to do with art or creativity as such. The critic really arises from the fact that creative activities wake us up and lead to knowing. The critic says, "Don't know, you might find out something awful about yourself, don't go into that river of life, you might drown." Actually, knowing is dangerous because it leads to change. Changes in perception, changes in how we live our life, changes in relationships raise fear. To live is to change. And no matter how positive the eventual outcome, change often evokes feelings of loss and even death. Many times we try to fight the critic with alcohol or drugs to increase our courage, or we try to deny its presence by overachieving or simply not trying at all. We are ashamed of our resistance, call it laziness or worse. We disparage ourselves for not succeeding, or call the safety of conventional life "success."

Instead, consider beginning to honor the resistance, consider getting to know the critic. The critic holds very valuable information. The critic holds our deepest fears; resistance shows us we are on the right track. If we shift our perception, our critic can be seen as trying to spare us the pain of change, the shame of fear. Our critic discourages us from doing things which are perceived as dangerous.

State your intention to get to know your critic. Acknowledge that while real people—parents, teachers, or others—may have criticized you, an internal version of the critic exists. The purpose here is not to affix blame, which only strengthens avoidance, but to meet the inner-critical-self aspect, which you have the power to change. Focusing on actual critical exchanges with others is a way to tap

Fig. 3. Critics *(ink).*

into the nature of your particular critic. Try to recall an instance of discouragement or criticism. Close your eyes and focus on the sensation, words, setting of the experience. Try to focus on the tenor of the voice and let an image arise. If it is a real person, let the image intensify until the personality is gone and the image prevails, for example, a witchlike teacher is no longer Mrs. Smith; rather, a witch is your image. Once the image is present, greet it and acknowledge any fears or other feelings. State your intention to make an image, and then do so: draw, paint, or sculpt the image, being as faithful to your inner image as possible.

Sit with this image of the critic. What fears does it mirror? Give your critic your attention. Try to receive its message. What sort of pain does it wish to protect you from ? When you are ready, state to yourself and your critic how much you are willing to risk. If hardly at all, say so. Thank your critic for the attempt to protect you. State your intention to be compassionate with your own fears, and vow to dialogue with your critic when it makes itself heard, recognizing that you can choose how much protection you really want and how much risk you will assume.

I found that I harbored an entire committee of critics (fig. 3). There's a nasty one who taps her foot and points to her watch. I'm wasting time when I create, she insists. But mostly my critics are laughing. I learned that being ridiculed, making mistakes, and not being taken seriously are among my worst fears. It is as if my critics are saying, "You? You think you have something to say? That's a laugh! You think you're entitled to that feeling of being so alive, ha!" We owe it to the world to be as alive as we can, to give what is unique in us to give. Art is a way of knowing our gift and learning how to give it.

Hang up your image of the critic. Now that it is outside you, you can develop a more conscious relationship. There will come a time when your critic will mature and change too, into a compassionate helper who lets you know when to keep working, when to sit and wait. For now, just try to accept your critic as is.

8

Knowing Background

I sit on my apartment building stoop, hoping that the phone company installer will arrive today, finally, after I've waited for three days. An old woman stops on her way in with groceries and leans toward me. "The last girl who lived in that basement apartment was raped," she says, close enough to my face for me to see her yellow, irregular teeth. "Keep your windows locked." It's stifling hot, but I feel a chill as she heaves herself up the steps. My father is no longer speaking to me since I transferred from a respectable college, leaving behind a full scholarship, to attend art school. No one in my family understands why I am doing this, and now that I'm doing it, neither do I.

The competitiveness of art school stuns me. It is not a safe place to experiment or explore. I am stuck in a constant fight with myself about art. What is the point of making pictures? To make art to hang in a gallery does not make sense to me. That is not my goal. But I can't come up with an alternative, and no one else seems to be asking such questions. I go through the motions, taking classes mostly in things I already know something about, figure drawing, painting, ceramics. Nowhere am I at home. I rarely feel that sense of immersion into process that I dimly remember about painting.

Whatever glimmer I had of art making as a way of seeing eludes me now. I need my eyes for seeing hazards—muggers on the street, lecherous teachers in critiques, and perhaps even, as my neighbor suggests, rapists in my tiny apartment. I dream of huge rats dancing outside my windows. Feeling unsafe prevents me from doing much work. The only place I risk anything is in a repetitive series of self-portraits, which I show to no one. My fellow students are in love with the idea of being an artist, and lots of time is spent on perfecting the role and the appearance. I do some of this too; I shop in thrift stores and tromp around in boots. But art school seems more like a place for practicing illusions than finding meaning.

Then I find her books. Books on art therapy that describe using art to enter and explore the unconscious, inner world. This makes sense to me, although I am not sure why. I assume the author, Margaret Naumburg, is dead because the books, which I find in the reference room of the Boston Public Library, are all out of print. Coincidentally one day, I overhear a woman talking to some other students in the school lobby, which doubles as a gallery and lounge. She says this old woman, Margaret Naumburg, is giving a seminar in the home of someone in Brookline. I accost this student and demand the details. I know she thinks me unspeakably rude (but later she becomes my best friend). The seminar is over, she says, but yes, Margaret Naumburg is alive and living in Boston, retired now from her teaching and art therapy practice in New York. I am overjoyed and write to Naumburg, pouring out my frustrations with art school and telling her I am deeply affected by her books. Several days later she calls and invites me over, suggesting I bring some of my art work.

"These are not the real you," the elderly woman sitting opposite me says firmly as she leafs through my portfolio of art school drawings. She is stocky and short with intense, watery blue eyes and a chirpy, birdlike voice. Her thin hair is in a bun, but wisps of it fly around her face and occasionally get caught in the side of her mouth. She brushes them away as she speaks. The ornate bracelets she wears clink as she turns over each drawing. I look at the series of self-portraits as she carefully regards each one. Tight, controlled renderings, head and shoulders only, with tentatively applied, fantastic color. The too-long neck conveys suffocation, the head strains to break free from an absent body. These drawings are not the real me, Naumburg says. I am relieved to hear that. I hope the real me, whatever that is, isn't as miserable as I look in the drawings. In the service of getting at this real me, she suggests that I try some techniques she

PERSONAL CONTENT

has developed to get at the inner world of unconscious feelings. Like Freud, Naumburg believes that fears and desires reside in the unconscious. Like Carl Jung, she also believes in universal symbols that connect all humankind.

I am to soak large watercolor paper in the bathtub, pin it upright to a board on an easel, use acrylic paints and big brushes, and paint away. Make a mark, she says, and see what happens. Let the painting paint itself. If I have a dream, all the better, use the same materials and put the dream down. I am grateful for these instructions, curiously more substantial than any I've gotten in art school so far. When I finish a painting, I am to write down my associations to it in a loose-leaf notebook. I am to divide each page roughly in half, the right side for my immediate responses, the other margin for future thoughts or insights. I leave Naumburg's place excited. Perhaps my reason for being in art school was to be present to overhear that conversation about her whereabouts.

That night I dream I am running along a beach. It is late afternoon, glowing with golden sunlight. I wear heavy winter clothes. Jack, a man I know, is further down the beach, tossing a ball in the air and catching it in a mitt. He is dressed all in blue and is facing away from me. The sand and sea melt together, sparkling gold, glittering surf, but overhead the sky is nearly obliterated by masses of black birds, flying, flying, in the opposite direction. At first the whole scene appears very beautiful, and I feel exhilarated and joyous. But there are too many birds in the sky and I cannot stop running. I feel out of control. Am I going mad? Jack turns and sees me but is oblivious to my danger. He yells out lightheartedly to me: "Watch out for the water." He is still quite far from me and can't tell that I am out of control. Finally, I fall down, screaming. Then I pass out of consciousness as the water lifts me up and pounds me back down against the sandy bottom. At last I cease struggling and the sea pulls me gently but insistently toward death, while the ceaseless flapping, flapping of the birds continues overhead.

When I finally struggle awake, I set about to follow Naumburg's instructions, amazed at the vividness of the dream images. I tear several sheets of watercolor paper from a pad and fill the tub with warm water. The surface of the paper softens as the water seeps into it. I set out a palette and squeeze out only a few colors: yellow ocher for the sand, several shades of blue, and black for the birds. With the paper on the easel, I begin to paint. I am not fully awake, still in the T-shirt I slept in. The dream holds me in its thrall. I put down a wash of ocher. The big brushes handle awkwardly. I feel the roll of the waves, hear them crash as I paint the sea. The birds are simple shapes, and I paint them quickly, overlapping the forms. I squeeze out a little brown and sketch in the two figures, me running and Jack tossing the ball in the air. I get a second sheet of paper to paint the next frame—there is a sequential sense to the dream that I must preserve. In this one the waves pull me under and Jack has turned in my direction.

I am back in the process of painting, powerfully led by the dream images instead of a live model as in the past. I am contained and directed by Naumburg's instructions. I connect to something that is full of energy. I finish a third painting, which is just the sand and sea with birds in the sky. The figures are gone. I lay down my brushes and collapse on the couch to look at the work. Slowly a sick feeling grows in the pit of my stomach as I regard the pieces before me pinned on the wall and still dripping. The power and vividness of the dream experience reduced to messy daubs and smears confronts me. My critic snorts in derision. Bringing such work to a critique would be suicidal; it is beyond amateurish-looking. Yet I can't deny the strength of the dream images nor the distinct feeling that I had connected to my inner world through painting them. I remember Naumburg's directions to write down my associations. I get out the notebook I had purchased for that purpose and begin to write, first a description of the work, then, in the wide left-hand margin, what I think it all means. I write: "I am reminded of my mother's death, which hovered like the birds for so long. For eight years she was sick and death was so often near. When she died I grew cold and numb like the water in the dream washing over me. I died then too, in a way . . . the feeling of being overshadowed by death is still with me,

There is nothing that can be fully enjoyed because at any moment death can end the happiness. Better, it seems, to be watchful than to enjoy." I also wrote: "I see the ocean as a source of constant renewal."

Writing in the notebook forms a lifeline for me from the smeary paintings to a sense of meaning. Paintings are supposed to speak for themselves, yet most of what I see around me in art school is mute and distant. We speak in words like "form," "gesture," and "surface," but no meaning, no content. The form of my paintings is weak; this is not "art" in any sense, but the meaning evoked by these images connects me once again, in a different way, to the river that surges below my observable daily life, the place of the soul. I throw my lot in with Naumburg and art therapy at that moment. She had given me something I hadn't found in art school: a reason to make images.

Over the next months I throw myself into using Naumburg's methods. I find the river. It is swirling, tumultuous, dark gray, unforgiving. I am dragged, gasping, through its twists and turns, caught in the gut by rocks concealed beneath its boiling surface. This is not what I expected. I paint and draw and discover that I am broken inside. I draw an image that recurs in my mind. I am filled with broken bottles. Now I am trying to walk after standing still for a long while, and the raw edges of the glass grate against each other and tear my guts. This is the price of clarity. The images I make draw out the pain, intensify it.

Naumburg teaches me the scribble drawing. Take a large sheet of paper, tape it to the wall. Close my eyes. Take a pastel chalk, any color, let it meander over the page in overlapping lines. Draw loosely from the shoulder, this is the body speaking, not just the hand, the body that has been mute since childhood. Open my eyes. See an image, use all the colors, add what's needed to render the image alive and in focus. A black scribble turns into an anguished girl, clutching her hands over her ears. I entitle this drawing *I Don't Want to Hear It* (fig. 4). In spite of her clutching hands I hear the reasoned voice of my father saying that my mother's illness is no excuse for poor

Fig. 4. Scribble Drawing: I Don't Want to Hear It *(pastel).*

grades. I hear the nun who clucks her tongue at me—"Don't be dramatic"—when I say I don't have a note from my mother when I am late for school. My mother, I say, is in a hospital, dying.

I draw a figure in a bed under a bright red blanket. She has long hair, her face is gaunt. She is me. I am dying my mother's death. Her eyes are empty, her soul is gone. On the wall are remnants, fragments, memorabilia of a life, a mask, a flash of color.

I don't want these images. They exhaust me, frighten me. Is it any better to have them out, on paper? I have coped until now by being very careful, making only small movements so that what is broken inside can't cut too deeply. The glass serves to guard these images from consciousness, like the glass that tops a barbed-wire fence. But this fenced enclosure is within me, is my core, fences me off from the river so I cannot get there.

I am a small purple figure clutched by a huge black hand that rises out of nowhere from the bottom of the page. I am struggling, straining to break free and reach upward toward life and light. My vision of the world beyond is in the upper corner, surrounded by a yellow line, keeping me out. The hand is powerful, graceful, even. I see it as depression, as mental illness. If I stop struggling, I will be lost to this black beast (fig. 5).

A black cat appears one night in my hallway, bushy, electric-looking, with bright yellow eyes. She ignores my efforts to shoo her out. She spooks me, staring intently at me and not moving. I shut the door with a shiver and paint an image to exorcise my fright. Later, when I go into the hall, the cat is gone. The image captures that stare, that cold regard.

In another drawing a colorful figure sits on a strange black chair. Her body is graceful and relaxed, but I think she may be crazy. Her relaxation is that of one who has surrendered the struggle to maintain a facade. Her face is multicolored, grinning. She holds a mask on a stick. The picture scares me yet there is something playful in its strangeness.

A painting begins with some strokes of black paint that turn into a pregnant bird. Her head is strained back; she is struggling to fly, but she is too heavy. She is falling into a fire. She is confused and doesn't want to die. The flames are faint and far away; she has a long way to fall. I see the bird as my mother, weighed down to destruction by her role as mother, which left room for little else. Yet I know that my mother loved her children. What if the bird is me? I want to fly away from being a woman, can't imagine being a mother. To be a woman is to die. My mother died. Women don't have choices. There is no escape for the bird. Her own weight, the weight of the life she carries within her drags her down to a flaming death.

All of these images and more emerge in six months' time. I enter my past through image making and see a speeded-up movie of the unacknowledged subtext of my childhood and adolescence. My mother is sick for many years. She suffers stoically, not wanting to inflict pain on others. My father devotes himself to her care and our survival. I am a responsible child, dutiful and very sad. Nothing is

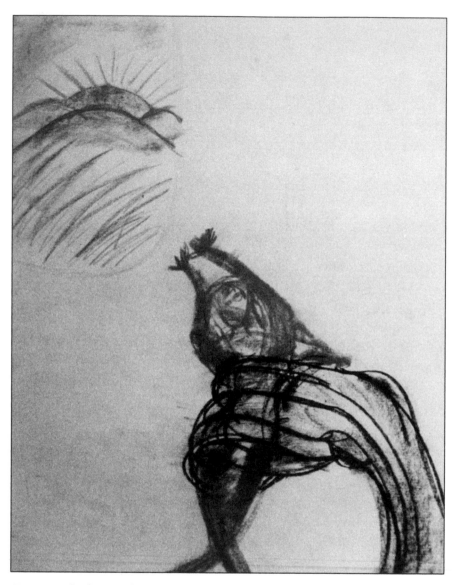

Fig. 5. Black Hand *(pastel).*

put into words. No one speaks of pain or fear, illness or death. Feelings are not expressed. Each one seems to be saving the other from pain by not speaking.

Consequently, I have no words for these images. I present them to Naumburg and she accepts them, which is some relief. But they are riddles to me. I have trouble deciphering the messages. All that is unexpressed is saved in the body, like a careful scrapbook. The body records what the mind denies. I don't know the language of the body, of feeling and intuition. I know how to think. But thinking unguided by sensation and feeling is a cold knife. Thinking about these images is scary. They mock my life of school and work and self-sufficiency. I think they say I am crazy underneath. I think they say I will never escape the clutches of depression. I think they say that being a woman is an inescapable death sentence.

Naumburg doesn't think I am crazy. I am afraid to ask her why. She thinks I should be an art therapist. I take her word for it. On the strength of Naumburg's belief in my destiny, I go to the work-study office of the art school and say I want a job as an art therapist. Someone called just that morning, the cheery woman in charge says, looking for an art therapist. The job is at an aftercare center, a program run in a church basement that provides service to people let out of the state hospital. Art therapy seems like a passport out of the dark, swirling waters of my river. Maybe I'd understand why these people are crazy and I'm not.

When personal content first begins to manifest, it can arrive in strange and cryptic forms. The methods described here allow you to enter under the surface of your everyday life. You will be able to see the contents of mind, in images where previously you may have had only vague feelings. Material in dreams, underlying feelings and fears, buried memories gradually take shape through images. It is important to remember that the image functions in the realm of metaphor, speaking powerfully yet symbolically. Do not mistake the message of the image for a literal report or rush to judge its content as meaning, definitively this or that. It is all right not to know at all in a cognitive way what an image means. You will make surprising discoveries, some delightful, other disturbing. To come to an absolute conclusion about an image is to rob it of its power as a guide.

Why bother to do this? Why risk disturbing yourself or your ideas about things? Contents of our mind, when left unexamined, exert a strong influence over our behavior. These unexamined contents are a source of our resistance to living fully and joyously. It is our fear that we will discover something terrible within ourselves that hinders our desire to know. We may have had difficult and painful experiences, and image work may reflect that to us, but ultimately it will also reflect that beyond any experiences we have had, however awful, is our soul, our essence, perfect and unassailable, our core. The soul's deepest wish is for us to see this and realize that it is this essence we have in common with all beings.

To know this is to become free of the power exerted by the contents of mind to limit us. To become familiar with our internalized past gives us a perspective; it becomes only one version of our story. Fears we had as children may no longer be necessary. Feelings which were unsafe to express may be painted and drawn and befriended. Remember that the image is the messenger of your soul and never comes to harm you. The misperception of the art school critique is that the image needs to be improved through criticism. The misperception of art therapy is that the image must be analyzed. Both approaches try to overpower the image with intellect. The image needs to be known, seen fully with loving attention and encouraged to speak, treated as you would treat an ambassador from a different world. Then it will develop and reveal itself according to its own logic.

It has taken many years to realize that the hand of darkness in figure 5 was the pull of my own soul returning me to my own center, the dark place of renewal. Trying to explain in words, I was limited to clinical concepts, black and depression suggesting illness rather than fertility and rebirth. The initial baptism in the river of soul was a painful start to knowing myself. It is my hope that by adding in the component of paying careful attention to bodily clues, by learning to honor and respect your own resistance, you will be able to work at a pace that suits you and gently undo the fears and misperceptions that keep you from fully knowing your true self.

Prepare your materials as you did for nonobjective wet-into-wet painting (see pages 28–30). Tape your heaviest paper to a board and wet it with a brush or spray bottle. Have your paints ready. Begin with a dream image. It can be recent or old, as long as some aspect of it is quite vivid. State your intention to know about the dream. Close your eyes and dwell a bit with the dream. When you have a clear starting point, a color or image, begin. The wet paper will reduce the clarity and render the image somewhat vaguely. Allow the paint and paper to be co-creators of the image with you. Notice whether more details come to you as you paint, or if something just needs to be in a certain part of the painting. Allow yourself to enjoy the painting process, trusting that by stating your intention, the content will manifest in the painting in the best possible way. When you feel finished, stop. If you have been stirred up by the process, clean your brushes and work area to restore a sense of calm. Ask your body what it needs. Are you ready to contemplate your image? Notice any resistance that comes up. Sit quietly and honor the resistance as a feeling. If it passes, sit quietly with your image and give it your attention. The image may seem like a visitor who speaks a different language. It may not feel as if it has anything to do with you. Notice what comes up as you look. Does your critic speak, as mine did in my first dream painting? Do feelings arise of fear, pleasure, curiosity? Just let them come and go.

Eventually, as you sit, you will come to know something. The process is like stirring up a mud puddle and waiting for the water to settle and clear. Once you get to the settled place, you are done for the time being, even if all you know is that you don't know anything about what the image is telling you. Part of the value of this work is in learning to watch yourself settle after being stirred up. Attending to this stirring and settling helps you know what really needs your attention and what is a distraction. If thoughts or ideas remain once you've settled, journal them. Don't worry about coming to a conclusion. The image process is a journey, and there is no singular meaning to an image. You will come to know it differently in the context of subsequent images.

Instead of wet painting, or if you have no dream at the moment to work with, try a scribble drawing. Tape an 18 by 24-inch piece of paper to your drawing board or to the wall. Standing, make some loose circles with your shoulders to relax. Then choose a pastel chalk, close your eyes, and dance it across the paper in meandering and overlapping lines. Open your eyes and state your intention to discover an image in your scribble. Feel free to turn the paper in any direction. Once you have found an image, use all the colors to bring it to life.

Observe your reactions. Do you resist seeing an image that seems silly or strange? Acknowledging these responses help you see what you might be denying yourself. Can you respond playfully if a "silly" image comes up? Do you want to correct or cover one that seems "strange"? These are simply things to notice, not to judge or struggle with. Sit with your scribble drawing. Recall that drawing is energy made visible. What sort of energy have you expressed? Stay with the colors and lines for a while, then let your awareness shift to the image. Consider what needs of your soul are expressed by the image. Does it need a story? Write one down if the image suggests it. Follow unlikely avenues. If a word or phrase comes to mind, jot it down, play with it, see where it goes.

Does the image want another image in response? Do you have a question for the image? Do another scribble or a free drawing with the intention of receiving an answer. Practice letting the image lead. You are learning to dance with your soul. What if you are stumped, blank, nothing clicks? Don't worry. When I worked with Naumburg, although I had little trouble accessing imagery, I could rarely talk about what I drew or even "free-associate." I think this was my soul's way of preventing me from intellectualizing and coming up with explanations for emotional experiences. Being without words was new for me and not very comfortable. I tried to write about the images, but when I look back, much of the writing pales in meaning, while after more than twenty years the images continue to speak and instruct me. They remain alive, and I get to know them even more deeply even now.

Because I believe in the process, I tried to do as Naumburg suggested and made many images when I may have been better off just sitting with one or two and letting the emotions wash over me. Instead, I detoured from my own process into becoming an art therapist, hoping in that way to make sense of all of this—intellectually, as usual. The crucial concept here is to come to know what is right for you, at this moment in your process. Honor any resistance, do not push through it heroically. There is no rush. Trust soul, trust image, and trust your own gut.

9

Knowing Work

I run art therapy groups three days a week for adults, most of whom carry the label of chronic schizophrenic. They are interesting people. Jim fancies himself a musician as well as an artist. He plays the harmonica and paints colorful self-portraits. His face is often bright red: he tells me that the Thorazine he takes to quiet his hallucinations makes him sensitive to the sun. In his portraits his face is often yellow. Robert's paintings are covered with phrases from the Bible. He wants to bring us all to Jesus Christ. He brings in liters of Coke and loaves of white bread to share, "to feed the hungry." When he gets caught up in his work, he has trouble staying on the paper, and his images spill over onto the table. Dave draws Volkswagens, always two, in a showroom window. When he's upset, he outlines them over and over until they vibrate with color. Alice draws bare-breasted women walking the dog and nude dancing girls and girlish self-portraits that depict herself before she got sick, when she was a promising actress.

I have no idea what I am doing. These people seem no stranger than many of my fellow art students. I provide art materials and listen as group members talk about their images. These people bear no resemblance to the definitions I read about in my psychology textbook. They look no different from people I sit next to on the train. Joe's red face could belong to a Boston dockworker as easily as to a former mental patient on a potent drug. It is their stories that set them apart. The way they make sense of life is not ordinary. To me it seems poetic and it touches me. I suggest they make pictures about the stories they tell. Like Tom, who came back from the Vietnam

War with a metal plate in his head. He thinks a man in New Hampshire, where he once worked as a cook, took his heart out and put it back the wrong way. That's why he doesn't feel right. In his painting, he leaves his head off and makes his heart really big. I hear Tom's stories as metaphors. My heart, too, has been misplaced, and I don't know what to do about it either.

All I do is listen to their stories. I don't really know what else to do. Sometimes I make images in the group, too, but less and less as time goes on. When one of the patients asks me for a date, my supervisor says I need to develop more professional distance. I am the therapist, she reminds me, they are the patients. Patients make art in art therapy, therapists make comments. I am lost between worlds. So many of my art school friends seem lost and undirected. How are they different from these "patients"? How am I different? I take my cues from my supervisors, competent, practical people who offer encouragement for my work. It seems like growing up.

Gradually I stop wearing my art school thrift store clothes and dress more professionally. I finish school and get a new hairstyle. I get offered a full-time job. In addition to running the art groups for the people like Dave and Tom who've spent time in the state hospital, I work with "regular people" doing "real therapy." I see people individually and get supervision from social workers and psychiatrists. I find I am pretty good at talking therapy. My supervisors teach me a great deal, but they don't know what to tell me about the art. Very few of the clients who come for individual therapy really want to draw or paint anyway. I work in an office with limited space and supplies for a fifty-minute hour. Talking seems more expedient. I learn to listen and reflect, to reality-test and empathize.

I want to work with kids and families. The clinic director says I need a master's degree. Everyone suggests social work as the practical choice. But I am uneasy; the art has already ebbed away from my work, and I have little time to do much of my own art work. I decide on an art therapy training program instead. I want to learn how to use the art more effectively. Besides, I've gotten so busy being an art therapist, I've forgotten all about the river. In an art therapy training program, I'll get to make art, reclaim myself as an artist, get back to the river. This job is just a brief detour. I imagine art therapy training will be like the work I did with Naumburg, except it will be done in a community of people making powerful images and coming to some self-understanding together. This time I'll understand it all much better, and it won't be so frightening.

In graduate school, I learn that therapy is something set apart and terribly private. The sort of image work I expect to do is not considered appropriate in a classroom situation. It is too messy, too unpredictable, too emotionally volatile. I suspect that few if any of my instructors have really done this sort of art work themselves. There is limited time to make art at all. Graudate school is about reading books, writing papers, studying. Graduate school is not about the river. The river is something you take care of on your own, if you even know it exists. The river will have to wait. But I learn something significant. I learn that both Carl Jung and Sigmund Freud developed their theories, which we study in some detail, by working with their own images: Freud analyzed his dreams; Jung used both his dreams and his drawings and paintings. They honed their ideas by working with patients, but it is in self-exploration that each man's most powerful ideas developed. They weren't crazy, although Jung especially seemed to realize that there is risk in images. It's not a process of total control. He talked about the need for stable supports in a regular life to anchor himself when he lowered down into the unconscious. I write a paper on this topic, drawing the parallel between these two men, that ends lamely by saying, "Somebody ought to do this in art therapy."

I graduate and go back to work with children and families. I am a full-fledged art therapist now. I teach and supervise and present papers at conferences. But I am farther away from the river than ever. I still run groups with Robert and Dave and all the rest. Jim seems to be doing especially well. His individual therapist says so. He finally has a job. He doesn't have as much time to come to art groups, and I miss him. He writes a poem for me when I finish school. A few weeks after he starts his job, he hangs himself. His mother finds him; he doesn't leave a note. We come together in the art group, patients and staff, wondering if we could have done more to help him.

Something was missing for Jim. Something is missing for me too. In spite of success as an art therapist, I feel a terrible void. I no longer even know that it's the river I am missing. I just feel edgy and empty. I think I want to change careers, write children's books. I take a course and the teacher asks why I want to give up such an interesting career. I resign my job and leave with my husband to travel for a while; after that, who knows? The technical term is burn out. I am hollow, empty, burned out. I have used up everything I have. Without the river to replenish me, I have nothing more to give.

Our work-self is one of the images we use to navigate in the outside world. For Jim, exchanging the image of mental patient for that of factory worker may have been more difficult than any of us realized. As a mental patient, after all, he had rights to art and poetry and playing the harmonica. By embracing the work image of art therapist, I was expressing my soul's wish to have some alignment between my inner and outer reality. My choice also bore the imprint of my father's voice saying that being an artist wasn't a real job. Our choices are influenced by our parent's dreams, teachers and other role models, our own early failures and successes. The stress placed in my home on education nudged me toward teaching art therapy in a university, the highest achievement my parents, whose formal education ended in high school, could imagine.

It is possible to wake up one day and find yourself with a highly evolved work-self without completely knowing how you got there, and wondering if it is right for you. Our work image, like any other of our lived images, is a constantly changing, evolving reality that develops out of our thoughts and perceptions about it. It can become more enjoyable if it develops along with our awareness of who we are and what we do best, or it can become a prison if it is formed largely in reaction to outside forces without our continually checking in with our soul and our gut. Imagine if each high school student considering a vocation were asked: how can you most pleasurably serve the world? Pleasure and work are not often used in the same sentence, yet as Suzi Gablik says, "our consistent thinking patterns create our experience. By changing our thinking we also change our experience" (1991: 23). By thinking of our work as a fixed entity, we guarantee that it must grow stale because we are ever-changing beings. By changing our thinking to consider work a fluid medium for our being to exist in, we open new possibilities. This is equally true whether your work is parenting small children, manual labor, or service of some kind.

Think of your work image as a boat that you guide across a waterway. There are forces besides your own tiller you need to be aware of. Your place in the stream is affected by the tides of the ocean and the storms at sea. There may be submerged icebergs or kelp waiting to curl around your rudder or larger ships passing that can flood your craft. Play with your image in your mind. Are you the captain of an ocean liner, imperial and majestic, or do you paddle a bark canoe deftly through white water? Are you in a rowboat in shark-infested seas or piloting a tugboat in safe harbor? Are you stuck in too small a pond in a craft that longs for open seas?

I once described my work image as me clinging to rotted pilings, the boat itself having broken up and washed away. It sounds scary, but once I let got and let the river carry me along for a while, it became an exhilarating experience of renewal. I eventually washed up on a sunny beach and set about to build a new boat by reinventing my professional self. An image I created when I began my new work with three friends, envisioning the Open Studio Project, shows a figure alone in a tiny dinghy, on the lookout for land or at least fellow travelers. The bird reminded me of the one in the story of Noah's Ark who returned to the boat because she found no land on which to rest. It also evokes the soul as a guide in the sometimes lonely journey to find right work (fig. 6).

Play with the boat image in your mind. Notice what sort of setting comes to you. Stay with the metaphor, the image. Are you

Fig. 6. Boat Sculpture *(painted clay).*

stuffed in the hold of a slave ship, waiting to get to a new homeland? Are you in a motorboat going too fast? Is there a crew, are you alone? Notice any resistance that comes up. If you can, just let it rise and fall and keep imagining. If it is too strong, pause and give it your attention. Write down your thoughts: "It's too scary to think about work," "I'm too old, too tired, too unskilled, to change," "I can't afford to change jobs," "I'm lucky to have work, better not think too hard about what's wrong," "I don't want to disappoint anyone," "I can't work outside my home without shortchanging my family," "I worked hard to get where I am; so what if I'm not happy? Who is?" Remember to honor your resistance; it intends to save you from danger, real or imagined, though it can also keep you stuck. If you are determined to know more about your work-self, take your time and go slow. State your intention to include letting go of resistance or having the courage to look at your situation honestly.

If you are intrigued by visualizing the boat and if work is an area you want to know more about, consider how you can create an image to help you focus on where you are now and where you want to be in the future. Sit quietly in your art space and form your intention. Make it as clear and direct as possible. It can be simple: "I want to see my present work image clearly" or "I want to create my ideal work image." Remember to add a statement to acknowledge your resistance, such as "I want the courage to look at my situation" or "I want to release any obstacles to seeing new options in my work."

Work is so freighted with extra meaning in our culture that it can be a challenging place to do image work. Yet for that very reason, making work the most pleasurable and satisfying it can be is a worthy goal. Changes in work are seemingly more public than inner changes; they affect family, our friends' perception of us, our self-perception, and so they feel riskier. Sometimes the image process yields the answer that just a small adjustment in work or a change in thinking is needed. A friend who is a wonderful artist who works a lot with fabric tried at one point to make sewing one-of-a-kind clothing her work. "What I did," she related, "was to self-employ myself in a sweatshop." Her deeply held inner idea of work did not include pleasure. What would the world be like if we each chose our work by asking ourselves, "How can I most pleasurably serve the world?"

10

Knowing Soul

We travel to Israel. I am in search of spiritual renewal. In Jerusalem I witness the yeshiva students marching joyfully to the Wailing Wall carrying their beloved Torah. I walk the Via Dolorosa to the mysterious darkness of the Church of the Holy Sepulchre and light a candle in memory of my mother. I hear the muezzin's call to prayer and visit the al-Aqsa mosque at the Dome of the Rock to pray surrounded by its glittering mosaics that disorient and transport me momentarily. In each place I discern doorways to the divine and realize sadly that none of them is mine. Jerusalem is alive with spirit, yet I do not find the river for myself in any of these sacred places.

It snows this winter, a rare occurrence in Israel. We are returning from Jerusalem to Kibbutz Ein Gedi on a dusty bus ride through the desert. Perhaps the communal life of the kibbutz is my answer. Suddenly as I stare out the bus window I see that the hills are flecked with color. The minuscule amount of precipitation has caused the desert to bloom. Tiny flowers dot the brown terrain, transforming the slumbering hills into a living landscape. How long have the seeds lain dormant in the sand, waiting for water and a chance to flower? How long have I been seeking the river and its waters of renewal? We cross the wadi, a dried-up river bed. The wadi is considered a dangerous passage. At any moment it is possible for water to rush down from high in the mountains and transform the wadi into a raging torrent that sweeps away everything in its path.

The wadi remains dry. We arrive at Kibbutz Ein Gedi safely. We are living here as volunteers to try out this way of life. Ein Gedi is situated on the Dead Sea. When I finish my work for the day, making soup in the kibbutz kitchen, I go to the sulphur springs, hot sulphur baths that bubble up out of the mountains. People come from all over Israel and Europe for the medicinal properties of the baths. I go there to rest my aching muscles but also to watch the women. I sit in the steamy, smelly water and watch the women. I watch them dress and undress. The women are mostly European and they are profoundly physically present in their bodies.

I watch a woman dress after her bath. She climbs slowly out of the spring. She dries her body unself-consciously, makes no effort to hide or cover herself. She takes her time. She is probably in her fifties. Her body, softened by time and the birth of children, has yielded to gravity's rounding. Her dressing appears to me as a sacred ritual of self-respect. She embodies the river. She moves with grace and dignity. I go to the baths whenever I can. When I return to my room I draw images of the women I see there. They lead me to something that is missing for me, like a half-remembered melody.

That I am compelled to draw reminds me that I seek the river through images. What I seek is within, yet I can't find my own way there. It is a dimly remembered dream. In the inward journey to the river, the images are my maps. What I need seems embodied in the women at the springs of Ein Gedi. I have been reading Joseph Campbell's books while on the kibbutz, especially *Hero with a Thousand Faces*. I begin to understand that what I am seeking has something to do with the feminine and that my soul is the soul of a woman.

For me, the soul and the river are inextricably bound up with the idea of God. I was raised in the Roman Catholic faith and loved the stories of creation, of Jesus, and of his mysterious and lowly birth. Throughout my childhood I read *Lives of the Saints for Every Day of the Year*. The heady scent of incense, the images of the Way of the Cross, the black-shrouded church, the open, empty tabernacle on Good Friday—these images embodied mystery rather than dogma for me.

By adolescence I was in an angry standoff with God. I taught Sunday school to the littlest children, where I could tell and retell the stories I loved, but I refused to go to Mass. What kind of God destroyed my mother with cancer? What kind of heartless imbeciles, priests and nuns and well-meaning aunts, tell a child that her suffering is "God's will"? But worst of all to me, what sort of religion provides only a sheeplike acceptance of such awful circumstances?

I needed to be angry with God, and found my way to the Jewish tradition through a need to express that anger. I needed Moses and Job, who struggle and doubt God. I converted to Judaism before my marriage. Although my husband was not religious, I needed a sacred context to contain our marriage.

Throwing myself into another tradition did not entirely answer my soul's need. My soul's need was sometimes embarrassing. To my surprise, I found that the images I grew up with, such as the crucifixion, were deeply embedded and continue to resonate within me. Eventually I realized that we do not choose images so much as we are chosen by them. The images are carriers of aspects of the soul's experience rather than symbols of religious dogma. The soul's remedy comes in letting the images convey their message directly.

We create our spiritual connection by attending to soul. Spirit enters when soul has made the place ready. Soul is basic, everyday, it is everything to do with daily life, eating, sleeping, loving, struggling. When we cultivate soul, our eyes become clear and soft. We see spirit and feel it, a sense of awe and reverence in many different situations, not only in designated places of worship. If our soul is well tended, we may even be able to enjoy and partake more fully in religious ritual and ceremony, to appreciate the diversity of expressions among different faiths.

What does your soul need to make the way ready for spirit to enter? Your key will be something that inspires in you feelings of reverence, the sharp intake of breath that we associate with awe. Beauty is a wonderful door to the soul. State your intention to yourself as clearly as possible. You can say, "What is my key to spirit?" You can say, "I open myself to awe today." Use whatever words feel right to you. Once you have clarified your intention, simply go about your day, planning some time during the end of the day to

---

reflect and be in your art space. If you have time, take a walk in nature where you let your eyes fall easily on your surroundings. There is no need to look actively for your key. It is best to try this on a day that you don't have pressing deadlines or weighty concerns.

When it is time for image making, sit quietly and let your mind settle and review your day. Pay attention to any subtle reactions you recall. There is an infinitude of things to see, but your eye will have been drawn to something particular. Perhaps it is the way two birds are sitting together on a wire. Maybe a cloud in an unusual shape speaks to you, or a baby's smile. Recognition of your key will cause a stirring; it may be very subtle or it may move you to tears. It may seem entirely unrelated to spiritual matters and be very ordinary. Looking into the eyes of a stranger or embracing a friend can be a key.

If an image comes to you, ask what form it wishes to take. Maybe it needs watery paints, maybe rich charcoal. Maybe it is an image primarily of color. Does it need words or does it want to remain only in your mind for now? Remember that creating an image is a way of taking action to make your intention manifest. The image increases the resonance within you and allows it to blossom and unfold and tell you its meaning. Trust your inner knowing and let the image instruct you. Be deliberately slow and also curious. Try to refrain from coming to conclusions; instead, follow your image like a trail of bread crumbs as far as you can. Then let it go. You won't learn everything at once. The image may take time to unfold its meaning. Let it sit on your wall for a while and just notice it as you go about your routine.

Thoughts and feelings may arise as well. When I began to observe the women at the baths in Ein Gedi, many feelings arose in me about body size, fat, aging. These were my culturally conditioned fears of the female body. The women I saw presented a new option, the female body as sacred. I watched, I made watercolor sketches from memory, I took photographs of women on the beach. Slowly I realized that my body would be my key. The soul prepares to enter where there has been suffering or neglect of an aspect of ourselves. Ask yourself where that place is in you.

If you find resistance rising at any point, let this task go and move on to another chapter. Don't be concerned; the key will be there when you are ready for it. Thinking in terms of spirit may raise arguments in your mind. Respect this and do not struggle. If you find conflict, wanting and not wanting to engage in this task, it may be useful to look more carefully at your resistance, not to change it necessarily, but to know it better. List beliefs you hold about spiritual matters: "I don't believe in what I can't see," "I believe in a loving presence in the universe," "God is a stupid idea." List your fears: "If I find God, I'll have to give up my life and join a religion." List any feelings you have, positive or negative, about spiritual or religious figures you have encountered. If any of these lists yields strong feeling, consider making an image. Like the inner critic, who can hold our creativity hostage, the inner apparitions of spiritual authority can block our connection to soul and spirit. It is not necessary for this to be so. Like every other aspect of our being, until we recognize our deeply held beliefs, we have no chance of freedom of choice. What seems like sophisticated rejection of spirituality may have originated in childhood disappointment with a religious figure now long forgotten. Images will reveal the nature of our relation to soul and spirit.

Knowing Story

We realize with some sadness that the kibbutz is not our answer. We return from traveling to settle in Chicago. I still toy with the idea of writing children's books, but when a large ad for an art therapist appears in the Sunday paper shortly after we return, I feel compelled to check it out. I get hired although at the interview I scarcely can string together any thoughts about art therapy that seem coherent to me.

I resolve to seek the river actively, methodically, not only for myself but to make some sense of how to work with art with other people as well. I feel like something of an imposter in my job, having not regained my moorings in art therapy but only come up with more doubt during my time away. At home I take out my sketches and small watercolors of the women at Ein Gedi. I stretch a canvas and plan a painting of a grouping of figures by the sea smeared with the special mud dug at the base of the sulphur springs. I work on the painting faithfully, but I am too far from the experience. The old voices return to criticize and taunt me: I don't know how to paint, the piece is badly composed, the colors are bad, the figures flat and static. I lose heart and put it away. The small sparks of what I felt at Ein Gedi are no match for the harsh winds of the inner critic.

At a loss for a right action, I remember Carl Jung's description of active imagination. He calls it "dreaming the dream onward." I want to go into my own depths, and not having any recent dreams, I choose an image that reflects my intention. Each night before I go to sleep I focus on the image of myself descending a staircase. I can only focus for a few minutes before falling asleep, but gradually, over a few nights, I notice more detail in the scene. The steps lead into a cave. A dim light flickers off the faceted rock surface. Off to the side on the cave floor is a booth; it is a teller's cage, like in a bank or a ticket booth at a carnival. I make out a figure with bowed head in the dimness before I drift off into sleep. In the morning I write down what I remember.

I am excited by this development and look forward to my next attempt. My beginning seems a bit trite and ham-handed, but I have no other way to begin and it seems to be working. The next time I move more easily down the steps and find myself standing in front of the teller's cage again. I notice the brass bars of the cage that glimmer in the darkness of the cave. It occurs to me to ask for directions. As I think this thought, the creature in the cage slowly lifts its head. I am face to face with a huge dark beast. It regards me with glowing eyes and I feel its warm breath. I turn and flee in absolute terror. It is a minute before I realize that I am lying in my own bed, my heart pounding.

Weeks pass before my courage returns to seek the dark beast again. I feel low and depressed, as if I could sleep and do nothing else. I do my job as an art therapist, in a hospital with alcoholics and acutely psychotic and depressed patients. I feel only partly available, as if some struggle is taking place below my consciousness that saps my energy. I wonder if I am chasing a chimera in my image work. I have a dream in which someone says, "Your glasses are dirty."

I decide to try again. This time I will do the image work during the day and draw the beast. I lie down comfortably on the couch and focus my mind's eye on the descending the staircase to the teller's cage. This image intrigues me because it connotes a bank and riches to be had, but it is also telling, and the "teller" is powerful but caged. Shortly, an image arises. I draw it quickly and write, as I did with Naumburg, in the red notebook. This time a story emerges. The beast is black and bound with heavy rope, but already I have terribly mixed feelings for him. His back to the viewer, he is painfully stooped, lashed down to a wooden docket, as if on trial for a crime. His huge, bushy head is bowed by the strain. It is unjust to bind him so. A deep pink-red glow surrounds him. His fire, even banked, gives off a great deal of warmth and energy. That's how he got tied up in the first place. It was feared that he would run amok. He is so sad, so tired, so misunderstood. All he can do is wait; he cannot free himself.

Next to him, paralyzed by fear, stands his keeper. She stares ahead with stoic discipline, but her eyes betray her fear. If she ignores the beast, she will remain safe. She tries to forget that she holds the key. Usually she forgets easily because she believes he is best kept locked up. At times she even imagines he is gone or never existed. This is dangerous imagining. At a deep level she knows that if the beast dies, she dies, too. Keeping him is her reason for living. At other moments, when she is tired or worn down, she tortures herself with the thought that she keeps him rather poorly. But she gave up her hands long ago so there is nothing she can do.

She can hardly bear the heat of him. His hot breath fills her with dread. The thudding of his heart deafens her. A thought, unbidden, seizes her: "I would rather die, explode in the conflagration of one embrace, than live on in this infernal coldness." She wishes for her hands to cover her ears, her eyes, to deny the thought.

In this one moment begins the unraveling of years of control. Moved along by the story, I make a second image. In this one the keeper turns to the right. As she does, the beast faces her head on. She realizes that the beast, like a mirror image, cannot turn unless she turns. All this time she thought he had a power entirely his own.

He faces her, his expression full of love but with such bestial coarseness, blunt and terrible, that she is struck still. His thick shoulders are raised in an effort to gain some relief from the tight ropes. It appears as if he has come up through the floor. Revolted, the keeper tears her gaze from him and looks down only to see her arms and hands restored: they have grown from her head, from her thinking of them, wishing for them. Her hands, warm purple, stretch out, in spite of her fear. Her mouth is set in a straight line, her lower body remains an ice-blue block. She is surrounded by a yellow haze; is it her own cowardly fear or the light of life returning to her? Her posture is ambivalence itself. She is drawn to the beast and repelled by him.

I am drawn to the active imagination process but repelled as well. What if I am getting in over my head? What if I am unleashing something destructive in myself, some mental illness? I am afraid and become too busy for a week or so to try again. Then a dream comes. I am sitting on a bench wearing only a skirt, holding an infant and trying to amuse him but feeling uncomfortable. He speaks to me, quite articulately, and with mild irritation tells me I must nurse him. I hesitate, though it seems quite obvious since I am unclothed on top. But I don't know if I want to be so intimate. Then I do nurse him, and a wonderful sense of rightness and completion comes over me. The dream seems to restate the problem of the active imagination in less frightening terms. I am reassured by the images of mother and child that by embracing the beast I will be accepting a holy union, rather than something bizarre, as I feared. The baby speaks articulately as the voice of inner wisdom within me. The beast conveys power, instinct, sensuality, darkness, parts that are foreign to me.

Convinced by the dream of the rightness of my work, I resume the active imagination. I lie down on the coach and review the story so far. The next image comes quickly and I get up to draw it. The beast is free of his ropes, gesturing toward the keeper, who has lost her features and is nearly a scribble. The beast becomes more defined: he is wearing a long black robe. His hands protrude, white and not very agile, rudimentary hands. His face is coarse with a wide, flat nose. He cannot see very well through his slitlike eyes, but he has several delicately formed mouths that blink and shine. He reaches toward the keeper, who is riveted in terror. It seems he will consume her.

In the next drawing he is poised to swallow her, not hungrily but sacramentally. His mouths open to reveal a black abyss. The red fire colors leave the beast to be replaced by green, red's complement. How will he be changed by this meal? The moment the beast is freed, the keeper is also freed, although freedom is not what she imagined it to be. Freedom means loss of structure, of outline but not really of form or identity. The energy is freed in the loss of the encumbering structure. The loss occurs when the beast is faced head-on. Both figures lose their bondage simultaneously and then lose their separateness by merging through the beast's act of consumption.

I meditate to receive the next image. The beast dies. I draw his arms crossed over his chest, his hands grasping his shoulders. His face is bluish gray. The black garment is replaced by a pale fawn-colored one. Behind him glow the hot colors on the right, cool colors on the left. The two figures have died together. It is as if the icy coldness of the keeper put out the fire of the beast, two extremes canceling each other out.

I don't know what this means; this seeming end to the story baffles me. But I have come down with the flu and have little energy to think about it. By the time I feel better, the Christmas holidays arrive with visits to family and friends. When I return to Chicago I note in my journal that I experienced a deep sense of comfort during my holiday visits. I return with a renewed sense of energy. I resolve to face whatever arises next in working with the images. The time spent deeply in the imaginal world delivered me to my family and holiday celebration. I participate there more fully than I ever re-member. Usually by the time I return from a family visit I am de-pleted and off balance. I believe I owe this change to the time spent dwelling in my inner space, as strange as it is. I have struck a momen-tary balance where the river seems to nourish all of my life and isn't just a place I seek in desperation.

I revisit the images once again, stretch out, close my eyes, and wait. Is there more to the story? Suddenly a horrible creature ambles into view, so I get up to draw. It is topped with a head that seems dead, deadly white with a huge trunklike nose. It has eye sockets but no mouth. The body is incongruously pink, with hints of rudimen-tary breasts. One arm extends off the page, the figure struggles to stand. The calcified head contrasts with the pink body, which has a newness, a lack of differentiation. The image continues to evolve. On the next page, the figure removes what turns out to be a mask

Fig. 7. Beast Series *(active imagination, pastel).*

by pushing it up on top of *her* head. For, although the figure is androgynous, it strikes me as feminine. The head has no hair, the face is peaceful and open, the body broad-shouldered. I think of a recovering cancer patient whose hair is just beginning to return after chemotherapy. She reaches off the page as if greeting someone. The mask looks small now. Whatever she is reaching for is connected to life.

I recall the picture I drew with Naumburg where the figure held the mask on a stick. The mask in the beast drawings is similar, though more grotesque. My fear then was that to remove my mask would be to risk insanity. This series done in active imagination suggests to me that the old image of myself as keeper of the fearful beast is indeed destroyed in the process of facing what is feared. Yet what arises out of that union is something new and perhaps eventually more whole. The mask still remains, as an artifact. The choice to accept the process of the river isn't always voluntary. I want to believe that the safety of the mask remains available (fig. 7).

Much later I make an actual mask based on that image. It is hard and bonelike; only the nose, the most primitive sense organ, is formed. It is as if a part of me was stopped, early on, from developing. It learned to breathe and so has survived, but not to see or speak. The active imagination series is a powerful one. It reveals that I must be broken and remade, perhaps many times, to come to awareness. I recall the painful tumult of the original work I did with Naumburg, encountering my own brokenness for the first time. I feel more able to endure this now, on firmer ground. Destruction of the old—old self-concepts, old defenses—must take place to free the new to be. Yet the old must be honored, like the bone mask, and not despised. My limitations remain a part of me alongside my potential. Still, what is this feminine self I seek who must be united with what is dark and neglected? Later still, on a page in my journal, I draw another image of the dark beast in charcoal, a messy material I wouldn't ordinarily choose to use in my journal, which contains mostly writing. In this drawing I am held, tiny and unseen, in the hand of the beast. It occurs to me that the beast is God, or at least a good and holy being. This seems preposterous and true at the same time.

Active imagination, dreaming the dream onward, is a way to reclaim your myth, your story. The soul narrates your deepest truth through image and metaphor. If you choose to undertake active imagination, be sure to take care of yourself in your ordinary life. Eat, sleep, and work regularly so that you have a set routine to balance the imaginal work. Do not attempt active imagination while using drugs or alcohol; this is both dangerous and dishonoring to the process.

It is helpful to establish a set time to engage in active imagination. I initially used the brief period before sleep because it felt safe; however, it also precludes drawing. Consider what feels comfortable to you. You must have uninterrupted time, so be sure to unplug the phone and minimize any other distractions before you begin. Paying attention to small details, such as sitting in the same chair or doing the active imagination at the same time each day, serves to contain the experience. There are several ways to record your experience.

You can visualize and then write it down, or draw when you are done or speak into a tape recorder as you visualize and listen to it later and then draw.

I found my story emerged in segments. I usually got one scene each time, which was a comfortable pace. By alternating drawing with visualization I may have slowed down the story's emergence. Find the method that is most comfortable for you. Keep in mind that the image comes to help and that it has information that you do not yet have consciously, although it is within you. Therefore, be as faithful as you can in rendering the image. Resist any urge to fix it up or to impose sense. Try not to interpret the story, but just receive it. If a narrative emerges, do not edit it for logic or try to finish the story prematurely. Use simple materials at first to get the images down. Later, if you want to work further, you can elaborate the images by creating masks, books, or story boxes.

Be sure to honor any fear that arises. If the images are frightening, relax and let the process go for a while, or in your next session ask the images to restate themselves. Honor your images. If you choose to share them with others, do so carefully and respectfully and only with someone you trust. Stay with the images through any twists and turns in the story. The purpose of active imagination is to show you things about yourself in a metaphoric fashion connected to your deepest self. Often you will be shown something of great importance that has been neglected in your conscious life. Once you get to know the shape and form of some of your inner characters, you will be able to establish lifelong relationships with them as inner guides who will gladly help you any time you are willing to travel inward to meet them.

If you wish to read more about the history and background of active imagination, consult some of the books listed in the bibliography at the end of this book (see Hannah 1981, Jung 1979, and Watkins 1984). Of particular interest is C. G. Jung: Word and Image, which contains an account of Jung's experience with active imagination, including images he created and used for personal guidance. Jung's theoretical work as based on his lifelong effort to convey the wisdom he received during active imagination and through his images.

Part Four *Deeper Waters*

Introduction

If you commit yourself to art as a way of knowing, a point will come when certain images appear which are "numinous" or spirit-filled. There may also be images that recur in various forms. This may happen right away or after a while. These images are signposts into the depths of your self. They begin to show you what your primary images are. Archetypal images emerge that help to place your personal experience within a larger context of the imagination of hu mankind. Following the lead of your images into mythology, literature, or writings on world religions or other cultures can help to instruct you in the deeper meaning of your work. These are additional forms of amplification.

Such images require witness. Finding the right context in which to share your images with others is an important part of the process. There are many forms of witness: the intimate sharing that occurs in a therapeutic relationship, collaborative relationships with one other artist, groups composed of fellow image makers, exhibitions of the work in special surroundings, whether a special spot at home, a gallery, or some institution you are affiliated with like a church, school, or library. The image instructs not only you but all who view it. It is also important for you to witness the work of others who are toiling in the same archetypal field. This can be done through books, as well as by visiting museums or traveling to far-off places as well as through the witness relationship. These images belong to all of us, or rather, we belong to them, and we are nourished by viewing images made by others that resonate within our depths. The idea of archetypal images and the nature of witness will be discussed further in the following chapters.

Knowing Archetypes

I set up a small room in our apartment to pursue the image journey. Sometimes the work is intense, sometimes playful. An image comes of a man standing at the entrance to a cave. He stands with his legs apart, his arms outstretched. He is old but vital, an energy radiates from him. He invites me into the cave while also shrugging his shoulders, as if to say: "You might as well come along; sooner or later you will." I have a sense he has been waiting to guide me.

I attend a lecture by an art therapist, Don Seiden. Instead of showing slides of patients' art work, as most art therapists do, he shows slides of his own work, which is personal, direct, from his soul. He is the first art therapist I encounter who is using the process for himself. I identify strongly with the struggle to understand the feminine that I perceive in his work. His courage to show his inner conflict inspires me. Up to now, I have shown my images to no one.

Don is a committed artist. He uses a range of materials, some sophisticated, like welded metal, and others very simple kitchen materials, like tape and aluminum foil. He seems to have transcended the artist role that demands identification with one medium in order to prove oneself. He has also escaped the art therapy truism that only "quick" work escapes the mind's censor and provides authentic inner work. Don's work is fully formed, surfaces richly embellished. He unites process and product in a way that shatters my limited concepts of how to work. Seeing Don's work frees me toward my own.

I do a scribble drawing shortly after his presentation and allow myself to pursue it to a fully finished state. It presents a woman in purdah (fig. 8). She wears an ornamental purple covering with a

Fig. 8. Woman in Purdah *(scribble drawing, pastel).*

jeweled centerpiece that streams down between her eyes. This streamer contains diamond-shaped mirrors that throw the viewer's own countenance back in fragments. The mirrors serve to confuse and distract. Her outward appearance is mysterious, ornate, and implies that she is dangerous and must be kept hidden. I try to make one of the scribble lines over her head into a snake, thinking surely she represents the Goddess, the divine feminine, and a snake is a worthy attribute. The paper simply refuses to accept the color I try to put down. Instead, the line becomes a rose and thorny vine twining overhead. Yet had I consciously chosen to draw a rose, I feel sure I would have fumbled. This is a strong experience of the image making the drawing. My guidance comes forcefully from the scribble itself.

I have the curious sensation in looking at the woman in purdah that I experience the feminine the way a man might, not as something I understand personally and identify with but rather as something outside of me, mysterious and threatening.

Shortly after this the old man from the cave appears in another drawing. He lies peacefully in a boat that looks like a big slipper. He looks comfortable reclining on colorful blankets and pillows. The front of the boat curves up. A black rose is drawn on the curve. The man has long white hair and gazes into the water, reaching toward a green fish. I have a quiet sense of being shown something important and of being on the right path.

I continue to use the scribble and work each drawing to completion. To stop short of completing the drawing on its own terms seems wrong. My inner critic seems thoroughly baffled by this approach. I sense that my critical facility is being re-formed in the process of making scribble drawings. The process becomes one of what works to complete the drawing, regardless of my personal preference. My conscious mind is not making the choices. Rather, the image itself dictates its needs. Perhaps if I had been more fully trained academically as an artist I could have overpowered the image by sheer force of skills. My detour into art therapy cut short my classroom art training. My conscious mind decided a snake belonged

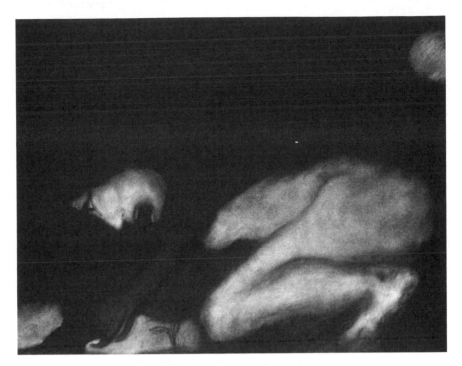

Fig. 9. Reflection *(scribble, pastel).*

over the woman in purdah but wasn't strong enough to overpower the image. I come to trust only what "works" visually on the image's terms.

The next scribble becomes a woman screaming at her own reflection in a pool of water (fig. 9). It is night, ink-black, and she is crouched down. A horse's leg is visible next to her. She is either turning into an animal or being mounted from behind by the horse. The image conveys a terror at union with instinct and reminds me uneasily of the previous beast drawings.

In another scribble a blond woman plays with the moon. She is curled up in a playful pose showing two faces, one coarse and voluptuous, and one cool blue. I am seeing a kaleidoscope of feminine images that both frighten and fascinate me. I recognize that I am being instructed but I don't really know what the images mean. Another scribble image emerges to speak about the union of opposites.

It has a central figure of a white bird who holds a red berry in its beak and clutches a brown rat with powerful talons. The background behind the bird is divided into a sun and morning sky on the left and a night sky and moon on the right. Since birds are usually either herbivores, eating plants, or carnivores, eating meat, the berry and rat symbolize something about a union of opposites that is echoed in the background. I have the curious sensation that I am not making these drawings. They come easily, as if I am dipping up clear water and pouring it into a cup. While the images intrigue me, I don't feel a sense of ownership or struggle that I do when I work on a portrait commission. I work on several commissions for coworkers at the hospital during the same period that feel workmanlike and, while enjoyable, come from a different place than the scribbles. I still employ the standard of what works visually with the portraits, but the decisions I make are more my "own." The portraits pull on actual images in front of me, while the scribbles seem to tap a more archetypal image "file" that isn't personally mine.

This archetypal quality inspires me to seek out a Jungian analyst for guidance in the image process. I am sure I need to work with a woman since so many of the images have to do with the feminine, and I realize I know little about the feminine, strange as this seems. I have valued masculine learning and achievements consciously while unconsciously disparaging women and secretly seeing myself as different than other women, critical of what I perceive as women's flightiness, shallowness, and lack of direction.

Through the local Jung Institute I find my way to Louise Bode, a woman analyst. I dream that a river runs through the center of Jerusalem, past the ancient hills and olive trees. I continue the scribble drawings. One becomes a magician who looks a great deal like one of the psychiatrists I work with at the hospital, brainy but remote. The magician seeks truth and holds a lighted staff. He is an expert, with all the trappings of authority. I recognize myself in him, I want to be a truth seeker, and to be seen as such. The next scribble is, without a question, the devil. His hand is outstretched as if to demand payment. What am I willing to pay for this image of the truth-seeker? Are these two sides to the therapist? I don't get to discuss it with Louise because as I show her the pieces and start to talk, I feel a sharp pain in my side. It is so strong it prevents me from speaking. I tell Louise and she suggests perhaps we can investigate the pain in a future session through some body work. This idea intrigues me but also makes me nervous. Before we can get to the body work, Louise decides to move to California. She suggests I continue my work with Lee Roloff, a male analyst. I am disappointed and wonder how I will ever learn about the feminine. I meet Lee briefly and we decide to make a start in September after we both return from various summer travels.

The woman rages, her dark hair flying. She pulls away from a light-haired child. The images of the two figures fuse, the child's stomach doubles as the woman's breast (fig. 10). I present this pastel drawing to begin my analysis with Lee Roloff. The art therapist in me worries that the drawing shows a terrible split. Although the drawing screams its content at the viewer, Lee responds to an area in the background, a bright red and magenta. "Try to discover what that color expresses for you," he says. I explain to him that my reason for entering analysis is twofold. I want to work out something about the feminine for myself, but I also want to learn firsthand, more deeply, how the image process serves as a way of knowing. I want to find a way to live with myself as an art therapist.

Before we left for Israel I was uneasy with the clinical approach to art therapy. Working in a Chicago hospital has only heightened my feelings of dismay. Patients stay briefly, usually highly medicated and without any follow-up except for their pills. There is even less chance to work with the images than I found in community mental health. Deciding what the image means seems to rob it of its power, yet this is what everyone, doctors and other staff, want to know. This is a riddle I want to solve.

Lee ignores the content of the drawing; this intrigues me. I accept his suggestion and simply shift my focus to the magenta, a rich,

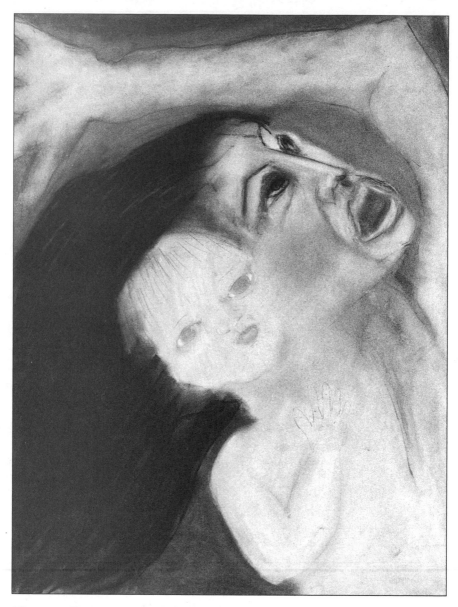

Fig. 10. Woman and Child *(scribble, pastel).*

pulsating hue surrounded by the red. I have no idea what it expresses. Just shifting the focus changes something. The art therapist in me stops in her tracks. She doesn't have to interpret, associate, or understand what the image means. It feels good. Something in me relaxes and makes space for the unkonwn.

Later in the day at home I have forgotten about the drawing. Lee's suggestion about the background, while intriguing, doesn't prompt me to any immediate action. While talking on the phone I begin to have a terrible pain in my right side. I get off the phone quickly and, remembering the pain I had when I showed the scribble drawings to Louise, decide to draw the pain. I sketch a vague outline of a right torso with flesh-colored chalk, just breast and pelvis indicated, the places where I experience the pain. Without thinking I choose various shades of bright pink, magenta, and bright red. As I draw, the pain intensifies. It gets so bad that I have to lie down on the floor. Gradually it subsides a bit and I resume drawing. Again the pain returns and worsens. I sketch a full torso to orient myself to the spreading sensation. The colors intensify. In a third sketch I make a nearly full but still amorphous figure. By now the pain radiates through my entire right side. I have never felt pain like this before. Moaning, I lie down on the floor of my closet to be in the dark, wondering what is going on and whether I am being ridiculous to draw pain instead of calling a doctor. I think about going to the bathroom to search for a painkiller, but I believe the pain has something to tell me—and besides, I can't get up. I've been on the floor breathing in the dark for about thirty minutes when the thought enters my mind to sculpt a baby out of clay. The pain has ebbed away to the edges of my consciousness. I get up and make some comfrey tea and return to my studio, a tiny glassed-in porch on the back of our apartment.

The pain is still present but less so as I begin to work the clay. I breathe deeply into the pain and the image sharpens. I work quickly to form an infant crying in anger and pain. As the piece takes shape, the pain gradually lessens. I work for forty-five minutes more, and by the end the pain is gone. I feel tired but satisfied and relaxed. I cover the piece with plastic to keep it moist so I can work more on the details tomorrow.

I get into bed, and while resting in that conscious but near-sleep state, I experience the crying baby both visually and kinesthetically. I see it, feel it, become it, especially the tiny clenched fists and mouth open in tearless squalling. What is this? Is it a memory? Was I left unattended when very small? I have a sense of reliving primary anger as a total body experience, blood pulsing, throat hoarse from wailing, muscles contracted and limbs flailing. *Being* anger, not just feeling angry.

After resting, I feel a great release. John and I go out to dinner later that night and discuss the baby. I have all sorts of associations to my mother and her passivity. She had to be mightily provoked to express anger, I recall. These "insights" seem hollow and somehow beside the point, though I feel compelled to try and understand where this infant comes from. I am struck by the fact that although I am familiar with clay from working in pottery, I have no training or experience in figure sculpture. Yet I had no thought about not heeding the call to make the image. Our dinner feels like a celebration of some kind.

I finish the sculpture over the next few days, savoring the process. When it dries I paint it with several coats of red acrylic paint. The finished infant looks slippery and newborn (fig. 11). I bring it to my next analytic session wrapped in a towel inside a shoe box. I make the connection between the magenta in the previous scribble drawing and the angry, untended baby. Lee is enamored of the image and honors it. But somehow the session is a letdown. The image feels miraculous, yet when I get angry in the session, when Lee takes a phone call and we run out of time, I am no more able to express my anger in the moment than ever before. Lee talks about how we will jointly parent the baby in the analysis. "Take good care of your baby," he says as I leave the session. The arm breaks later on that night. I repair it in tears. I am frustrated at his imperfect understanding and my own inability to express my misgivings.

What is the purpose of the imagery? Is it a separate, parallel proc-

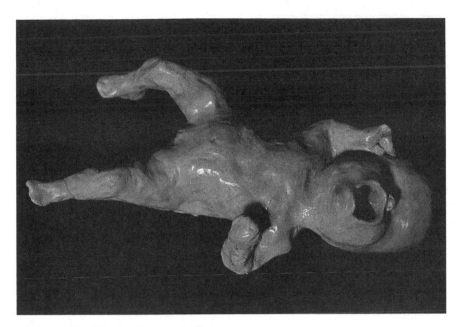

Fig. 11. Red Baby *(painted clay).*

ess to the relationship with the therapist? In art therapy the image is supposed to provide the common ground where the therapist and client meet. I recognize the red baby as an expression of my unmet needs, but so what? I do a drawing later about my inability to express the anger I feel in the present. Daggers of red and pink thrust upward toward my blue elongated neck and clenched jaw (fig. 12). I make a free painting of a torso that turns into a face. It, too, is in bright shades of red and pink. These different images suggest that reality is a hologram. I exist in the present both as a screaming infant and an adult who chokes back anger and as a segmented torso with a belly that is a vortex of rage. Separate pieces, kept apart for survival's sake. The images present me with a fuller spectrum of my reality, more than can be accommodated in the confines of the analytic hour. None of these images are apparent on the surface; I seem to be an utterly ordinary and reasonable, even-tempered person.

I make a scribble drawing that is profoundly disturbing to me. A frowning older woman with a grotesquely exaggerated left eye stares

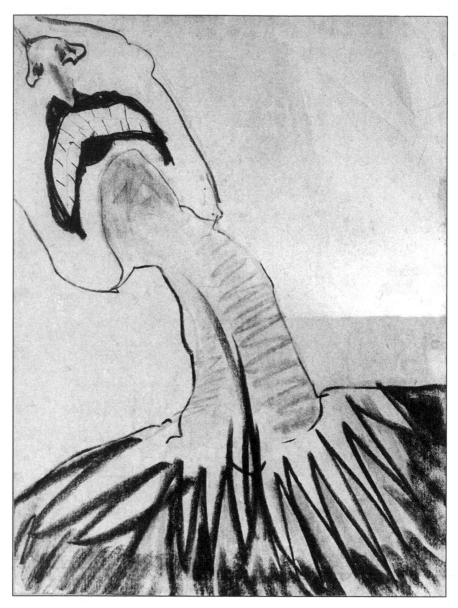

Fig. 12. Anger Held In *(pastel).*

out of the page. Her shoulders shrug upward, and a slight hand gesture conveys a sense of hopelessness. She has bright red lips and a frilly blouse and seems the archetypal frigid old maid. She wears a few emblems of the feminine, but she is a bitter imposter. Most disturbing are her "legs" and "shoes," which form a tight circle evoking a protectively locked vagina. She wears a black wig covering wisps of her own hair; she reminds me of Orthodox Jewish women who cover their own hair with wigs. (I have always been intrigued by the idea of the Orthodox wife who covers her hair and prays separately from men so as not to distract her husband from study and prayer. I don't know any such women, but the image evokes for me taboos against the feminine that are internalized in me as suppression of anything that could distract or weaken the intellect.) She is the horrible specter of the "strong" woman who chooses work over love; she has locked up the aspect of herself up that forms relationships. I have received the advice from several women mentors to concentrate on work, that relationships are ultimately disappointing for intelligent women. She says, bitterly, "Don't bother with the feminine, it isn't worth it." I am relieved when Lee asks to borrow the drawing and puts it away. He will not help me with the negative aspects of the feminine. He doesn't say so, but this is what plays out in our work. Uneasily I recognize myself in this figure. I have a great deal to undo if I am to fully embrace the feminine. A part of me also believes that women who are "feminine" are less able, less smart, less capable. Up to this point I have been relentlessly focused on my career and very ambitious. This figure is a chilling glimpse of where that road can lead. My "orthodoxy" has to do with women being strong and self-sufficient, in reaction to the "weak" woman of my mother's generation.

I make a series of collage paintings on shirt cardboard of women as saints. These women present meals or hold up cleaning supplies as if they are sacraments. I recognize these women as well. In spite of my career aspirations I also hold deeply ingrained beliefs about what a woman is supposed to do. Cooking and cleaning and caring for others are part of it; satisfying work is in addition to these tasks, not instead of. These are not wholly conscious expectations, which makes them harder to question. The final image in this series states the problem clearly. A woman in saintly garb kneels before a male "angel" with huge powerful wings wearing a sinister trickster's expression (fig. 13). With a shock I see myself mirrored in this painting. Within myself the feminine is subservient, yielding to the promise of protection from the masculine. I have identified with male values at the expense of feminine ones, which seem weak and sickly to me. The paradox is that in actual relationships I appear quite strong and on perfectly equal footing with men. I have prided myself on not getting into the sort of petty struggles that I observe other women having with men. This portrait of my internal "marriage of opposites" stuns me. I feel cheated and tricked. I don't yet know what reclaiming the feminine will look like or how it will change my life, but I want to know.

We move out of the city into a near suburb. I have a room for a studio, and I paint as much of it red as possible. It begins to feel like a womb, and I like being in it. I find a red armchair in a thrift store and spray-paint my easel red.

Image making and analysis are feeling rather mixed up. I am not so sure they really work together. I do a drawing of a baby on the lap of the beast, now green, who is reading her a story from a magenta book. I recognize this drawing as a reflection of the transference relationship. The analysis had something of the quality of the idealized bond between the father and a little girl. I feel secure there, seeing the images of my journey in a storybook, but the analyst is doing the reading. In fact he suggests working out my feelings about the relationship using these images in a storybook form. But something is not quite right about this picture. The child needs to go forth and live the images, not simply have them safely read to her from a book. The image restates for me that the analysis in a way is another version of my inner split. The analyst stands for the masculine as a benign force, and the feminine is no longer grown to a sickly and passive adulthood but is restored as a child to relive and reclaim her power as a female. It comes to me that whatever the

Fig. 13. Saint and Trickster *(gouache on cardboard).*

images are that will grow from this picture, they need to be oil paintings. Oil paint is the medium I have studied most, and though far from having mastered it, I feel it is somehow serious and important. The story must be contained in very reliable and sturdy form; this much and nothing else, I know.

Even after creating powerful images of long-held anger, I wasn't instantly freed to express angry feelings in the moment. I never showed the drawing in figure 12 to my analyst. It was too obvious and too consciously connected to a real incident, his taking a phone call during our session where I brought the red baby sculpture. Instead, I rationalized that he had honored the baby and that my angry feelings about the interruption were trivial—typically "feminine" behavior, feeling hurt because a man's attention is distracted from me: behavior that I had internalized without knowing it. The image of the frowning older woman has taken years to grasp, and she continues to speak to me. She is saying that relationship isn't worth it, it isn't possible to really be oneself, with all the messiness of emotion and feeling, so don't even bother, wear the clothes, play the role as needed, but the reality of what it means to be a woman is just too much to take.

I only began slowly to see how my identification with the masculine was a fraud. These splintered pieces of the self served me well for a long time. Giving them up is not an easy job. The fact also remained that to feel and express anger as a woman, I needed an image of that possibility. I had yet to find the image I needed. We need new images if we are to change, images of other possibilities. I believe that the soul contains infinite possibilities. First, the existing images we are using to operate must be recognized. If they are no longer effective, they must be mourned and given up. This is scary and difficult but required of us at each change in our life stage.

During this stage I was able to share and discuss these images with my husband and with a few women friends and students who related to the images. This enabled me to begin to incorporate more range in my self-image as a woman. Looking at images of myself as an art therapist and teacher was much harder. I began to question my values of rationality and control. I felt rather inept at moments as a teacher and therapist. I had no close colleagues at the time with whom I could honestly share my struggles. The art work potentiated and contained my inner turmoil. I was yet to see what trials lay ahead for the little baby who so far sat easily in the comforting lap of the beast, eager to read the story of her true self.

Certain images are "yours" to be expressed in your particular way while also having more universal significance. Holding both the personal and the universal aspects of the image requires practice and support; it is a dance, an ongoing alternation between the large and the small. There are pitfalls in becoming one-sided in either direction. Traditional therapists and even some art therapists tend to focus mostly on the personal meaning of an image. Jungians and archetypal psychologists have a rich view of the cultural and universal aspects of images but sometimes lose sight of the significance of an archetypal figure for the actual life of an individual. It is important to keep in mind that these images have an autonomous existence, a message to convey not only to you but to others as well. When we respond to "great" art it is because the artist was able to express something we feel as a deep truth. The idea of artists as individuals who perform this expressive task for society is part of the hero myth that we, as the human race, are outgrowing. Joseph Campbell points out that the genius of Michelangelo is that he powerfully expressed the dominant guiding myth of his society. We are living through the transformation of the myth of the powerful father authority figure. This is a time of transition. In such times everyone is needed to bring forth new guiding images as the old ones wither away. New images are emerging in every aspects of life. Science gives us the Gaia hypothesis, physics describes life as a unified field, medicine discovers the inner healer and the mind-body connection.

In a time of transition, when outer image guides are no longer in place, whether in the form of agreed-upon enemies like the Soviet Union or female role models in the form of one idealized body type, each person must look within to find their way. Image making is a way to accomplish this.

State your intention to explore the roles you have internalized without full realization. It may be helpful to make a list first, giving title to the images you intend to create such as the good mother, the sexy woman, the leader, the conquering hero, whatever roles you have played or even those you observe in others. Begin with an image that appeals to you, that may be enjoyable to explore. Use whatever material seems compatible. Feel free to enhance the archetypal aspect of this task by also using pictures from books, magazines, or other sources. Using a photo as a starting point or the image of a particular woman who personifies the role you seek to explore can help. Take your time to accumulate and create a range of images.

When you have a good variety, review your images. Spread them out and see if there is an image that seems numinous or mysterious to you. Hang up an image or images and state your intention as a willingness to dance with your image back and forth between the personal and the archetypal. Choose the most compelling image and decide to dialogue with him or her. Like active imagination, dialoguing occurs in a state of light reverie. Ask the image to tell you what it knows. Let the image hang on the wall where you will see it for several days. Work with the personal meaning of what you learn. Write down everything you can think of. You may get new insights, or you may notice you are restating a lot of material that you already know.

Let the image sit out a while longer. Let the personal meaning sink in or fade away. Then consider what you might do to explore the archetypal dimension of your image. Jung called archetypes "forms without content." Think of an outline for a vaguely female figure, which is then filled in by your experiences of feminine individuals—mother, sister, daughter, grandmother, teachers, friends,—to eventually comprise your experience of the archetypal feminine. If your experience is narrowly or rigidly defined, your possibilities of how to be are limited. Making these images conscious allows them to shift, enlarge. When the forms remain unconscious, our behavior is driven by unseen forces. While much of our experience of archetypes can be seen in dreams and images, we also unconsciously live out our archetypal contents in our actual relationships. We find partners who carry an opposite charge and get into relationships where the expectations are fixed rather than fluid. The reason for dwelling in these archetypes is that the Self or soul contains all possibilities. The more we explore, the closer we come to understanding the multiplicity of being. We can begin to understand others who may be stuck in a particular and limiting role. Our empathy and compassion for ourselves and others grow. When we see how all possibilities—kindness, cruelty, achievement, lethargy, generosity, greed—exist in everyone, we can let go of the need to label others in order to keep our image of self wholly positive. Blindness to multiplicity leads to scapegoating and persecution of differences because we fear otherness in ourselves and tend to want to destroy others who seem different.

Allow this exploration to nourish you and perhaps spark more image making, keeping the process alive and dancing. If it feels like schoolwork or drudgery, let it go. As with many of the tasks described in this book, you may find yourself going back and forth between different options, some deeper, some just for relaxation and centering. The wonder of the image process is that it supports us at the level of need we have at any moment if approached with intention and attention.

Knowing the Dance

I am living parallel stories. Working in the image process reveals that life is a series of multiple, overlapping realities, quite distinct from one another while also intertwining. Consciousness tends to limit my perception, to edit out seemingly unrelated details. But the river that flows beneath all life is rich and multifaceted. The simultaneity of these realities is hard to grasp.

Images emerge. I make a mask of the bonelike face from the earlier beast series (fig. 14). I don't actually decide to make the mask; rather, it is the mask that decides to be made. I notice when rereading my journal that it is exactly one year since those drawings where the mask first appeared were made. What does the incubation of this image mean? In my analysis I talk about my marriage, my wish to have a baby, my fear of pregnancy, my fear that in having lost my mother I am forever maimed somehow in all things having to do with being a woman.

I think about the image process. Images absorb my anxiety, resist my interpretation, take me places. Initially I seem to quest for a metaphor, and once a strong one appears, some healing begins. Often the metaphor is fragmentary, a small gestalt within my being that grows in signficance over time. Like the bone face mask. It was a drawing; now, a year later, it is a dimensional object that I can pick up and turn over in my hands. I can only allow it to be, acknowledge that it comes through me, to me, and trust that at some point I will learn its purpose.

I notice that images tend to be repetitive and to permeate my life. The trick seems to be just to hold the image in awareness, not

Fig. 14. Bone Face Mask *(Celluclay).*

rush prematurely to meaning, to closure. Otherwise the image fades away, ineffable and lost to me, until the next time it reappears in a slightly altered guise, triggered by events or other unknown factors. I am on some middle path connecting what is inside me, through image making, to something greater than myself. Something universal, profound, more evolved, an intelligence that I seem to communicate with through the images. I also worry that this is grandiose and I am being dramatic.

My father comes to stay with us for the Thanksgiving holiday. It's been years since he and I have lived under the same roof. We visit at the homes of relatives when I come to town. I get up in the morning and find him drinking a glass of wine for breakfast. It's no different from having orange juice, he says. That detail pierces the bubble of denial I have lived in all my life. I speak to him about his alcoholism, say that I can't be with him when he is drinking. This is like detonating a bomb in my family. My brother says it's not really a problem, plenty of people drink more than Dad. My sister is afraid my words will cause more harm than good. After my dad goes home, life proceeds. The river washes over all of it; all of it is the river.

I make three pastel images of my father after his visit. They are chilling, yet the quality of the drawing modulates the pain of content. A part of me stands back and admires the line, the colors, the power. Through the images I am transported into and then through the tears and rage that consume me during the days following his visit when the reality of his alcoholism seeps into my awareness like the pain of a previously ignored injury. The rage I feel is indescribable. The images portray waste, death, entrapment in vanity and weakness. Living with these images helps.

Showing the pictures to my analyst helps, too. Not his interpretations, his associations to Oedipus in the eyeless image, but rather the quality of witness. He witnesses my perception of my father's darkness. In making the images I admit that I see my father's shadow. By bearing witness to the images, Lee sees this too, and doesn't turn away. This seeing without recoiling is what undoes judgment, I think. If I look long enough, can I get to forgiveness? Lee doesn't urge me to see the light in my father, he doesn't deny the power of the darkness. We don't search for its cause. He doesn't condemn my father and he doesn't condemn or praise me for my work. He is an informed witness who knows something about dark and light and shadow. He knows and I come to know that everything is about dark and light and shadow. There is no use in denying one or the other.

Looking back I see that confronting my father and giving up an idealized version of him led to insights about myself. The portraits showed me attributes I had denied in him: arrogance, a kind of cold superiority, and a calculating quality of acting out of strategy and self-protection rather than honestly and from the heart. These same traits, I realized, were beneath my strength, competence, and rationality. I had idealized my own self-sufficiency, not seeing that it was also a form of mistrust and isolation. These are not pleasant things to confront and certainly not qualities I like to see in myself. I needed a shift in my inner values to allow myself to embrace relatedness, to trust that I could act from my heart and survive, to let others see my needs. I focused more at the time on my admiration for the portraits as drawings.

I could see in my father an unwillingness to admit any "weakness," which is what admitting to alcoholism would have forced him to do. I was still unable to acknowledge any vulnerability in myself at this point. The images allowed me instead to see the isolation required by my father to maintain his self-image. I was yet to face my own isolation.

When working in depth, images will transport you back and forth between the past and the present, the self and other, the personal and the archetypal. You will gain insight into your own life but also, if you look closely, into the greater context of time, place, and politics. My father is my personal father and also represents to me the father myth of our culture where patriarchal values dictate that weakness is unacceptable in a man. The reason for doing this work is that the larger fabric of values in a culture only shifts incrementally, as individuals do the difficult work of changing themselves. Moving from a hierarchical model of society to an egalitarian one cannot be achieved through legislation alone. The change must take place within the hearts and minds of individuals.

To facilitate this learning, consider the idea of witness. Think of someone who can dance with you back and forth between the personal and archetypal realm. Choose this person carefully, someone whom you can trust and who shares your willingness to explore. Explain the idea of attention, intention, and witness. To witness is to see and affirm. It is a skill. It involves putting aside any personal agenda. The witness does not judge, criticize, extol, reject, or evaluate your images. To witness is to be-with. The witness is changed in this being-with, enlarged by witnessing the unfamiliar or strengthened by witnessing the resonate. Be aware of your own wishes. Having someone witness your images is not the same as therapy; it does not involve coming to a diagnosis or problem solving. Having someone witness your images will not instantly right all wrongs of childhood, save a marriage, or ignite a romance. Yet witnessing is a powerful form of connection and works best when there is clarity between the two parties and a willingness to attend to whatever happens.

Choose an image or two that you wish to share. Invite your witness to join you after explaining the process. Spend a few minutes together attending to the images in silence. Share your intention with your witness. What do you want to ask of the image, what do you want to know? Then allow the process to unfold. What do you want from your witness? It is up to you to decide how much discussion is needed and on what aspects of the image or related subjects, or whether a simple silent time will do. Do you want the witness to share feelings and reactions?

You serve as the director and decide when the process is finished or choose a prearranged amount of time agreed to both parties. You may decide that you and the witness will act by making more images in response to the one you have chosen. Together you decide whether the relationship is one you will maintain in an ongoing way. If you choose someone who also makes images or does other creative work, perhaps you will decide to alternate the role of witness and receiver. Each relationship is unique and must unfold in its own way.

Knowing Patterns

I begin the series of oil paintings based on the sketch of the child on the beast's lap. In the choosing to make this painting, the image already changes from the passive child in the warm lap. In the first painting, the beast wakes the child from sleep. A vulturelike fire bird perches on the headboard of the child's bed. Other ghostly spirits play around the room. The beast brings light, which floods through the open door. The child gazes straight into the eyes of the beast, unafraid—delighted, in fact. The beast says, "Come, it's time for you to go." The creature of the dark brings light. This image begins the mystery series of the child paintings.

These paintings demand stretched canvas, carefully primed, and oil paints that are viscous yet can create intense luminosity. I apply paint with layers of tinted glazes, adding just a little paint to a wash of linseed oil and damar varnish. This medium has a rich, heady smell that I love. Layer after layer eventually builds up the image with its illusion of dimensionality.

In the second painting the child sits on the beast's shoulder, holding the beast's green fur tightly with tiny fingers. I am overwhelmed with a kinesthetic pleasure in painting this gesture. To know the beast, I must go as a child. The bird leads the way as they leave the bedroom to enter the light. The child's head is turned back toward the room, delighting in the novel perspective of seeing things from the beast's vantage. What awaits beyond the light is unknown.

In the third painting, the beast cradles the child in its furry arms and makes its way across a wide expanse toward a cave. The fire bird perches above the entrance to the cave from which the light flows.

Cypress trees cast shadows in the moonlight. The other spirits frolic in the night.

Once inside the cave, the child is spooned the light substance itself from a bowl by the beast. The beast has brought the child this far and the bird is impatient for the journey to begin. The child eagerly takes the substance in the cozy surroundings of the cave. The bird pecks at the child's head as if to hurry things along.

What are these paintings? Each emerges from a pencil sketch, the next sketch done once the previous painting is under way. I do not exercise any cognitive choice about the content or how the story proceeds. All I do is try to stay with what works in terms of the image. In this way the process is similar to active imagination.

The fifth image shocks me. I think at first it is out of sync with what has gone before. The child is face to face with a towering blue woman-mother-saint. She indoctrinates the child into blue cold pain and suffering through which sanctity is attained. The child, naked and small, contrasts with the woman robed in blue, voluminous and overwhelming. While the child stands mesmerized, death reaches out from within its hiding place in the woman's robes to close its bony fingers over the child and claim her. The child's former guides, the beast and bird, are nowhere to be seen. Or have they just shifted shapes to provide this vision?

The blue figure wears a mask and points to her hand, wounded with the stigmata. Her robes define a void where beckoning death lurks. If the child enters, she will die or become like the woman, a skeleton in mask and robe, a puppet of the unconscious. The figure represents the option for the child to self-destruct to attain sainthood, to endure the passive yet powerful course of self-denial. She is an illusion thrown up to the child to instruct her in the feminine, what she must meet if she is to continue her mythic journey and achieve a true self.

My journal notes a confluence of events around the time this painting was made. I feel a permeating sense of doom and look at my life to seek the cause. I start with work. I iron out some dissatisfaction with my schedule at the hospital. I speak to my colleague at the university where I am teaching and process some difficulties we experience together. Still, the sense of doom remains. Then I note the date and realize that late February is the anniversary of a difficult time, the days that preceded my mother's death. I remember: she is at home and suffering from an inoperable brain tumor that has not responded to any treatment. She refuses narcotic painkillers because of the hallucinatory side effects she experiences. She drifts in and out of consciousness, unable to find a comfortable position. She asks my father if she is dying. He doesn't answer, but tears stream silently down his face. I am astonished by her question; it seems to me she has been dying, slowly, piece by piece, for the eight years since her cancer first began. A few days after asking the question, she dies.

Without conscious intent, I am painting the sixth image in the child series. The child is pushing the feminine figure into a raging whirlpool. The child refuses initiation into the pain and martyrdom offered by the figure. The figure's pious mask slips away and reveals that death itself, all along, has been trying to seduce the child.

Loneliness engulfs me following this image. I can't begin the next painting. Weeks pass, the loneliness prevails. I wonder more about the image process. Perhaps the aesthetic gratification is primary when the work of the images is to integrate something very painful. The slow process of oil painting ensures that I can maintain balance and function in my outward life during the mythic journey of the images. The child series contains difficult material, the conscious and unconscious teachings I have received, from family and religion, about what it means to be a woman. I outwardly cope with the feminine by avoiding its depth. Outright rejection seems a terrible risk. Yet the paintings "work"; they have an imaginal integrity that sustains me in a time of sad aloneness.

Then a mask emerges. I spend hours forming a Plasticene mold to form the mask. She is an old familiar figure, vicious, sharp-tongued but calling it truth-saying, in the cruelest way. She has never had a face before. I encounter her in other women I know who reject the soft part of the feminine, and all too often I have seen her in myself. The mask is time-consuming. After sculpting the features,

I apply layers of soaked torn newspaper along with glue, which dry and form the mask (fig. 15). Like the bone face mask, this blue woman is an artifact that washes up from the river in dimensional form. She has not been wholly conscious in me. I try to control my sarcasm and sharp tongue. But my anger leaks out from beneath my pious good-girl mask. While I am sculpting the form, I get a phone call from an angry colleague who is nearly deranged because of a perceived slight. The extremity of her anger ignites my own; I feel refreshed by the honest if blunt exchange.

Months pass, dreams and other issues fill the analytic hours. What is to become the seventh and final painting in the child series sits unfinished on the red easel. I dream of participating in a masked dragon dance, a slow, undulating ritual. I dream I am pregnant and about to deliver amid a group of women at the home of a midwife. Two older women relatives of one of the mothers-to-be walk around and, seeing bloodstains on the carpet, cluck disapprovingly.

I feel ready to complete the final painting. I think I know what it needs. So far the child kneels by a blood-red pool. The child is alone after the destruction of the world. This death lasts years and years. I believe a white flower will bloom in the blood-red pool. I want life to come out of this death. But I am depressed and I have an intense pressure in my chest. The pain binding my heart is very strong. There is no time in the heart: every wound is new, and un-shed tears mount there with unhowled screams, anger fierce as dogs' teeth wild with the kill. How can I unleash all of this? Is it really possible for images, mere paper and paint, to contain it?

I dream that I arrive at a store at exactly five o'clock to buy an art therapy book. I think, "Perhaps they will sell it to me even though it is late." I get in the door, but the women, who are preparing to close, ignore me. One locks the door. I get the book and ask to be let out through the door, but they say no. "If you want to go out, you have to go the back way." They show me to a back door that opens onto a basement full of stuff, dark and crowded. The entrance is blocked and no door is in sight. I become angry with the woman and say, "I don't want to go that way." She shrugs. I realize I can go

Fig. 15. Blue Mask *(papier-mâché).*

that way but it would be a pain. My path in art therapy will be through the dark and crowded basement.

I have been working on an article for an art therapy journal. An esteemed colleague known for his own sharp tongue reads it for me. He says it is "vituperative." I realize that the blue woman wrote the paper, unleashing her spite and venom, criticizing art therapists for faults that I also share. Her angry words are wounding but offer no constructive alternative.

I dream I am recovering from amnesia. In the dream, to orient myself, I kneel down and draw a figure of a woman with colored chalk on a blacktop driveway. At my analyst's suggestion, I do this drawing on black paper, like the driveway. A moon-faced blonde looms up with outstretched arms and wild yellow hair. She is too big for the paper; I can't fit her lower legs and feet on. I resist this moon-faced figure. I try a free drawing in response to the resistance. A tiny figure leans on a wall between a voluptuous dancing blond woman and a slack-tongued monster rising out of a gold vessel. I identify with the small figure, who appears quite overwhelmed. I fear the forces of the instinctual feminine, which I have invited into my life without really knowing the consequences.

Over the next two days I work on another drawing, a scribble that becomes another blond woman, nursing a baby. She is another, more formed version of the figure in the dream and free drawing. As in the beast series, the monster is replaced by an infant who happily suckles at the woman's ample breasts. This is a vastly different relationship of the child to the feminine, not the fearful indoctrination of the blue figure. Is it she who awaits the sad child kneeling by the side of the blood-red pool? This blond figure is so physically different from me, light and voluptuous while I am dark and thin, that it seems clear she represents an archetype within me, an image of the divine in a form I need to have. Meeting the old inner image of woman as harridan, male imposter, bitter and cruel, have made space for the nurturing potential to be called forth.

Still, all the child has known, her legacy, is gone. She remains kneeling by the pool of blood, mourning her loss. The painting is deeply red, the red of blood, rage, sorrow, and pain. The painting also becomes darker and darker until only a golden glow remains around the child in the devastated landscape. A vague mask sinks into the pool and the child watches it go.

It is only after many years had passed, after I had read a considerable amount of literature on shamanism, that a workable metaphor for the mystery series images emerged. The ingestion of a substance and the terrifying visions that follow are a common element of initiation into the shamanic or mythic world. This mythic world exists within everyone but isn't usually accessed. When I made the paintings I was not at all clear about their message. In fact, I exhibited the whole series in a show entitled "Pictures without a Story" at the C. G. Jung Center in Evanston, Illinois, as part of my doctoral work. I invited viewers to write their own versions of the story they saw—a form of witness, although at that time I wasn't yet using the word or the idea of witnessing. While some comments were helpful, I had to wait for my own awareness to ripen before the story could anchor itself in consciousness.

The mystery paintings showed me one version of my story. In it I am led into the dark to be initiated with light and find the source of forgotten feelings. At the base of the anger is grief and loss. Accepting these images, even without full understanding, allows the next facet of the feminine to surface: voluptuous, full, nurturing. She represents vulnerabilities I never saw as a real part of myself. The compassion she radiates can only surface after vindictiveness and rage have been allowed to the surface.

Finally I began to see that anger has been there all along, unacknowledged, in me, in the pious nuns, even in my saintly mother. The mask of the blue woman jumped out of the painting into 3-D form in the mask. She represents the sharp-tongued means through which my anger, and the anger of many women, leaks out, not directly but in gossip, unkindness, and sarcasm.

The paintings demanded certain materials, oil paint and canvas. This spoke to me about the seriousness of these images, the soul was demanding my attention, saying this is major work, pay attention. At the same time, the form and craft made them easier to share in a public forum; they served as a rehearsal for relating to the work as my true self, the beginning of understanding the need for witness.

Five years after the paintings were completed, I was receiving a massage. During the course of the treatment I saw in my mind's eye the last painting, the child kneeling by the red pool. Then I saw the child rise slowly and walk away. I understood this as a message that on a deep level I continued to mourn my own mother. I felt released to allow something else to replace my long-held grief. I mark this experience as a milestone of my spiritual development.

These paintings now hang on the walls of the stairway down into my basement studio, where I continue to explore my own images as well as work with others and their images.

Our personal myth is so deeply embedded in us that it is difficult to see, yet we live out of it every day. Our myth is what generates the patterns of our behavior, how we respond to others, our expectations of life. Our patterns are repeated in ways small and large throughout our existence. Noticing our patterns, without judging or struggling to change them, is part of image work. State your intention to know a version of your myth, realizing that there may be many versions. Image it as an archetypal tale, seen through the eyes of your child self. Begin by recalling your earliest memory or memory fragment. Make that image in whatever medium it requires. You can consider it an amulet or key to the rest of the story.

Then, using active imagination to suggest a character or plot beginning, allow that image to lead you forward into a story. For now, don't be concerned about whether the story confirms or denies any of the "facts" of your life. Let go of the actual people, names, and events. Move into the realm of the image and its patterns, and let a tale emerge. Once your story comes to a stopping point, see if you can think of a form that can contain the images. It may be a book that you make; it may be a series of drawings or story boxes. This story is your epic poem, and it may take a long time to complete.

Maybe it needs words or music; maybe it will be a drama that needs to be performed. Trust the image to guide you to the methods that you need. You may find you need to learn a particular method or technique of image making. This step corresponds to the preparation for a mythic task that characters often undergo in tales. A teacher or mentor may come into your life. Keep open to all possibilities.

Honor this process in its imaginal state, and it will lead you to new understandings. Consider along the way what sort of witnessing is needed. Originally, members of a community shared a basic myth and witnessing occurred in the form of periodic ritual. You can create new rituals and new communities where stories are once again held sacred. Don't rush or push—this is your life unfolding. Your job is to notice and enjoy the image process even when difficult feelings arise. See them but let them go. Do whatever is necessary to take care of yourself while you are engaged in this work.

15

Knowing Life

I draw a boy in a forest, looking up, startled by a sound. He stops as if hailed by a voice from the distant past. I prepare four large masonite panels and begin another series of oil paintings. I paint a lizard-headed creature watched by a coarse man in formal clothes. A staircase divides the figures. A rose lies on one of the stairs. I think of my early attempts at active imagination, descending the staircase into the depths. I resist the paintings; I don't know what I am doing with them. There are three. In one the figures talk together on a park bench. In the third they are marrying, or so it seems. I work on them for several weeks, but I can't resolve the face of the man, and so finally I scrub it out with turpentine and put the paintings away, unfinished. I never use the fourth panel at all.

I don't like the masonite anyway. The surface is hard and un-yielding. The paint smears around but doesn't really take to the surface and transform it like it does on canvas. The panels resist my efforts, don't meet me halfway. The paint slips around and only runs if I thin it with turpentine. There is no subtlety. Why can't I just be a painter in what seems like the normal way? I can't choose a subject matter and then work diligently and follow it through, producing a body of work that can make some kind of sense hanging in a gallery. All I can do is wait to be seized by an image, muddle around with it until it stops speaking to me. Then I wait, feeling impotent and hopeless. Although the waiting and confusion I have experienced with past images has always given way to meaning at some point, that is no consolation in the present moment of despair.

I draw a figure crouched beneath the corner of the universe, spiritual energy swirling around and above. Yet the figure is in a desert outside of the life force. I visit a psychic who says I will struggle with God this year.

I dream of a beautiful baby and learn that I am pregnant. It is fall. This was our plan, work things out so I have the baby in May, after my teaching is finished, take off the summer, and then return to work in September. I have thoughts of a soft sculpture I want to make, but I find myself intensely resistant to going into the studio. I also resist the idea of continuing analysis. The long drive wearies me, yet I feel inconclusive, unfinished.

Pregnancy plunges me into a heightened state of sensory awareness and physicality. Pleasurable sensations such as making love and eating are more so. Even the feel and texture of clothing is enhanced. John treats me as if I am especially precious. I am easily fatigued and give in readily to sleep. I am surprised at feeling comfortable with the changes in my body, the heaviness, quietness. I grow reflective and feel my thoughts and ambitions ebb away. Before, I have sought these heightened sensations, this feeling of being alive and in the river in image making. Now I simply am living in a higher key. The need to make images isn't as pressing.

My energy is drawn upstairs into the light, to sewing and making things for the baby. I don't paint; I make dresses, a quilt, a bathrobe. The studio feels large and cold and alien. I attend a workshop titled "The Pregnancy of the Therapist" and make a drawing that is all body, round and full with no head. An unmarried friend expresses alarm when I show her the piece. "Don't lose your head, don't lose your mind!" she warns me. As though everything I am is on some bargaining block. A baby for your power, Rumpelstiltskin. I have plenty of energy for work, I'm not worried. I am jaunty about her concerns. I have been increased by pregnancy. I feel favored by the Goddess, initiated into her mysteries, a woman at last. I feel powerful and am convinced I have crossed a threshold beyond which my doubts cannot follow.

The month of my due date I am distracted, unsettled, desiring to turn inward. The next steps of my career loom before me: doctoral work, research, writing, the demands of the academic work I have chosen. A colleague and I have a paper accepted by an international journal. Will I find that having a child supersedes all of this? I can't imagine that. I have always been a planner, and this is my plan. But I am alternately tired and driven with energy. Can I do more? Maybe my friend is right and I'll end up in a housedress and slippers, shuffling around my house with a vacuum cleaner, my books and paints forgotten. I have seen women in the park, staring into nothing as their children play nearby. The thought chills me. Suddenly I feel like a cocky child strapped into the front seat of a roller coaster in that terrifying moment when the ride reaches the crest of the first big hill. Like the child in the mystery paintings who eagerly eats the light and receives visions not bargained for. How will the little being I am about to birth change my plans, my life?

Two days past my due date, I dream that my belly is translucent and I can see the baby's hand and foot as they press up against the confining space. I do several drawings of this magical state (fig. 16). I make a plaster cast of my torso. None of these pieces has a head. I teach my last classes of the semester, turn in my grades. Everything is proceeding according to plan. I am ready. I take the train downtown; walking, I have heard, is supposed to induce labor.

Pregnancy is the river. I am immersed in life in a way I have never been before, in the physicality that overwhelms thought. I have shifted from a thinking to a sensing being. It is a powerful state in which I am more open to the world, delighted by the sights and sounds around me. Impatient, the day before Adina's birth, I draw myself giving birth to her, hoping for magic.

The birth is strong and quick. John is there, and he bathes Adina minutes after she is born. He reflects back awe and wonder to me. Like countless women before me, I hold my beautiful child and put aside the pain. I am triumphant, complete, proud. Adina, with her little mop of dark hair, resembles the birth drawing I did.

It is months before I find my way back to my journal and into the studio. Childbirth and its aftermath are oceanic. I remember my childhood dream of being caught in a tidal wave, my first painting

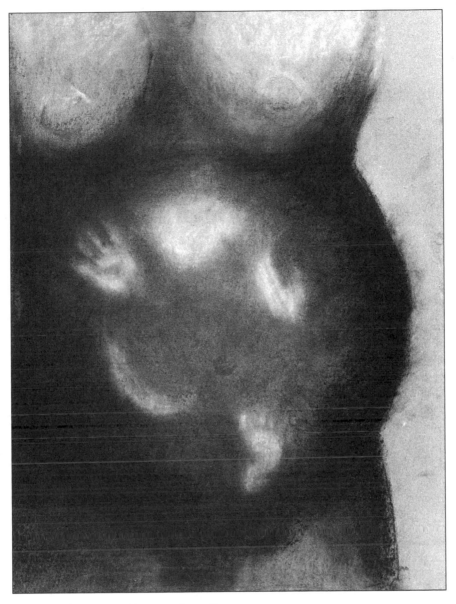

Fig. 16. Pregnant Dream *(pastel).*

with Naumburg of the relentless ocean, and recall that at about age eight or nine I was actually pulled under by the waves one summer while playing at the beach on the Jersey shore. In my memory I fight and fight, and only when I am so tired that I stop fighting do the waves deliver me onto the shore, exhausted but whole.

Pregnancy and especially labor and the birth have been this way; forces that I can't fight. Once more I am delivered onto the shore, exhausted but whole, yet wholly different. Will I ever regain my sense of a separate self? Will the body I finally felt was mine ever be mine again? Will I return to making images to thread my way through the overwhelming image of the mother? Will I be able to rely again on image making to know who I am?

I did return to teaching in September as I planned. Separating from Adina was painful. I cried all the way to work for the first week or two. I only went to campus twice a week, which made it bearable. I was also working on planning and organizing a professional conference and contemplating a Ph.D. program, necessary if I intended to remain in academia. I was happy and busy. If my art and writing were haphazard, well, my day-to-day life was rich and full. John admired my ability to mother our baby and confirmed my sense that I was doing a good job.

Life was focused outwardly, as it needed to be as I adjusted to many new demands. The role of mother felt comfortable and exciting, almost euphorically so. The image work I had done so far enabled me to embrace and enjoy my daughter and husband in this new family we made. I imagined I was done with painful image work; I had solved my lingering problems. I lost sight once again, as I had when I got my first art therapy job, with the ongoing need to stay in touch with the river, with the internal life of the soul. I felt strong and capable and couldn't imagine feeling any other way. I had support in my life for being a mother, a group of other women with babies the same age. We met weekly to talk and share and let the babies play together. It wasn't until six months later, when the river once again overflowed its banks, that I was led back into the image-making process and the next learning I needed to do. The three paintings of the lizard-headed woman stayed stowed away, unfinished and still a riddle.

Strong physical experiences are another entry into the image process. While pregnancy is especially powerful and served to evoke images in me, there are many other physical experiences that can do the same. The trick is to remain conscious and aware, to give attention to the phenomena we experience. We know life through our bodies, so that when physical sensation gets our attention, other means of experience can easily fall away. The body can provide entry to the soul or distraction from it.

For women, our menstrual cycle provides powerful images of transformation and the wheel of life. We have become enculturated to virtually ignore this rich source of images, though at one time in the ancient past women gathered together for numinous ritual. The menstrual taboo originated in the power of this sign of blood. We who hurry on with our lives neglect a monthly opportunity to meditate on the cycle of all life. By ignoring or despising our physical sensation, we reject a source of wisdom.

For both men and women, experiences of physical exertion—running a foot race, cycling long distances, diving, rock climbing—can evoke images. Pain, illness, and injury also provide opportunities for shifts of consciousness that yield images. Often these physical cues come to bring us a message that we have otherwise declined to hear. Considering pain as an image that comes through the body allows us to consider different solutions besides simply taking painkilling medicine. Focusing directly on the pain, having the experience rather than running from it, is often a more successful solution to pain relief.

A knee injury I sustained while skiing a few years ago put me on the couch for several weeks. In the enforced solitude and stillness, images of frustration and helplessness gave way to an image of vulnerability expressed in a small sculpture of an open heart. I began by despising my fall and clumsiness. Only gradually did the experience of being "broken" lead to the realization that only through our brokenness can we let others in to share our life.

Recall your own physical history, from childhood to the present. Notice what you remember. How were illnesses or injuries or physical events like puberty treated in your life? Your intention is to use physical experience as a way of knowing. Take your time until one particular experience comes to mind. It can be a simple present experience like a headache or menstrual cramps or a profound event like surgery or a broken bone. Notice all the memories that come to mind, the place, circumstances, the reactions of others. Let your mind shift into image gear. What images come to mind? Once the image is clear, create it in whatever medium seems right. You are using image making to clarify and amplify the memory of a physical experience.

When you are done, hang up the image. Consider that your body has something to tell you through pain and discomfort. It can be something as simple as asking for more rest or as complex as suggesting a whole new way of life. Ask your body to witness your image, and pay close attention to your physical responses as you give your attention to the image. Consider sharing your experience with your health-care professional if you are under treatment. Often, doing this work can shift our perception of a physical illness or injury and allow new possibilities to emerge.

If you are someone who rarely pays attention to your body, consider keeping a somatic image journal for a week. At the same time each day, use art materials to create an image of your immediate bodily sensation. If you are a very verbal type, skip journaling and just record the images. At the end of the week, notice whether you feel different. Notice what sort of themes appear in your drawings. Do they change as the week progresses?

16

Knowing Grief

It is November of 1983. I am traveling to New Jersey to see my father, who is gravely ill. I don't want to go. I am caught up in my own life, teaching graduate art therapy students, taking care of a new baby, anticipating a busy holiday season. Besides, we aren't on very good terms. It's been about one year since I confronted my father for the first time about his drinking. I spoke the word "alcoholic" out loud to him. I faced the person he had become after so many years of alcohol abuse: out of touch with those around him, repeating the same stories over and over, bitter and critical. My father, a bright, funny, loving man, ebbed away over the years on a sea of gin. Finally his condition worsened past the threshold of my denial.

The confrontation didn't help. I say "alcoholic" but he hears "bum." It is a heartbreaking standoff. Christmas at my sister's is grueling that year. He is confused and wounded by her ambivalent refusal to serve him a drink. She is trying to follow my lead, hoping our actions will urge him to get help. I am not that optimistic. I just know I can't sit in the thick gray fog anymore, pretending to converse with him.

I arrive in New Jersey possessed by the fantasy that Adina, my baby, can magically restore my father to the man he was in my childhood, full of stories and playful humor. Holding this precious infant will redeem him.

I enter the hospital room, dim and cool, shades drawn against the brilliant afternoon sun. He looks weak, shrunken, but clear, his hazel eyes luminous. I ask if he wants to see Adina. I am sure I can get the nurses to let me bring her in, and if not I am determined to smuggle her in under my coat. "No," he says. How could he not want to see her? I'm hurt, angry; he is no less obstinate than ever.

"You don't want to see her?"

"No."

Slowly, over the next days as I sit there beside his bed, reality— *his* reality—catches up with me. I see a man working at dying. All the fog fallen away, the pretense, layers of disappointment and self-doubt. My father is dying his death. He reminds me of Adina in his helplessness and openness. He's not scared at all, as if he'd always known what death would be like. He's not joking, jibing, complaining. Can we only be open when we have no choice? No, there is always a choice. There is a stillness in this room that I am drawn to. I look forward to coming to the hospital. We talk a little about his childhood, the house he grew up in, his mother, who died before I was born. None of this is about me, I realize. None of how he was was ever about me, or any of us. He was formed by his own beginnings, like everyone else. I remember something my mother used to say before she died of cancer many years before: "Dying ain't as easy as it looks." I repeat this to my father and he smiles. I ask him to tell my mother about Adina, feeling at once crazy and comforted. He nods. I feel myself soften toward him during my visits as he has softened toward himself or toward what lies ahead. I wish I could maintain the openness I feel when I am with him. I feel ashamed at my arrogance when I have explained him away with my diagnostic flair. I experience something like simultaneity. He is still who he is; he hasn't become a saint. The pain he caused himself and others did take place, but it's been forgiven, I think, not denied. This forgiveness is nothing I've done or not done. I am just a witness here in a timeless instant.

When I was a child, my father took my brothers and me to the woods near our home to play and explore on Sunday mornings after church. He is off into the woods now, alone this time. I stand at the edge of the forest, yearning somehow for the completion I believe he is going toward. I begin to understand why he can't hold Adina. She is a passionate tie to life, and he is untying his bonds to this life.

She is what keeps me on the edge of the forest, able to turn back to daily conflicts and joys. He must walk on into the forest. I return to my sister's house and nurse Adina, who sucks noisily, taking in life with happy hunger, then dozing in my lap amid the dinner preparations in the busy kitchen. Holding her here in the simple heart of life, it is I who am redeemed.

My father died in early December. I felt more joy than sorrow at the funeral. Relatives I've avoided for years hold Adina and tell me about myself at her age. I am knitted back into the fabric of my extended family, momentarily at least, aware of my life stretching backward into my own childhood. Food and laughter and memories are shared in the tiny, tired house in which I grew up. This scene echoes the best memories I have. My father would have enjoyed this party.

Returning for Christmas that year, I feel closer to my family, deeply at peace. His death and how he died gave us that. Like many kinds of pain, I see the pain of his last years more clearly now that it is ended. He was a ghost in my life for a long time, caught up in his own mazes. Something of what was lost seems restored in my father's dying.

After the holidays I return home to Chicago's unrelieved winter grayness to resume teaching, the daily routine of home and work. I expect the lessons I learned at my father's bedside to remain as obvious to me as if they'd been tattooed onto my skin. I try to incorporate some of what I know into my application to a doctoral program in which I must design a course of study. I will look at how art reflects and mediates these profound life passages, birth and death. I call a local hospice program to see about a possible internship. The nurse in charge is skeptical but agrees to meet with me. They usually don't accept volunteers with such a recent loss. I assure her it was an exceptional death, and well grieved.

Within my busy plans I am slightly depressed, I have a cold, lose my voice. It's normal, I tell myself, it's winter, the letdown after the holidays. I keep up with my schedule, but the lethargy drags on. I've lost the calm sureness and sense of peace I felt. To care for Adina is an effort, teaching is laborious. Maybe it's more than a cold. I decide to get a checkup, maybe I'm sick. I describe my symptoms to my doctor, who has a bright-eyed, very pregnant medical student in tow. I say that I am tired a lot, not much interested in sex, not really enjoying anything. She asks about life changes. I mention Adina, six months old, my father's death, and burst into tears. She is sympathetic and hands me a box of tissues. Her words have unleashed feelings of sadness, denied in my busyness. It is a relief to cry; I didn't cry much at the wake or the funeral; I felt so peaceful then.

The doctor looks concerned as my tears show no sign of abating. "Are you wishing you could be with your father?" she says solemnly, then turns to the medical student and says, "I'm assessing her for suicidal thoughts." How dare she? I damn well know the symptoms of suicidal depression. My tears stop, I feel my body rigid with rage. I wipe my eyes. "I am a therapist," I say evenly, "and I am *not* suicidal." I am angry at myself for showing my feelings, furious with the doctor for turning me into an object lesson on the perils lurking in a routine physical. I want to report her ham-handed bedside manner, but I am ashamed of my grief and tears, as if as a therapist I should know better. She offers me a referral to the psychologist. I coldly decline. I leave there shaken by the doctor's imperfect empathy, depleted by my own weary, defensive response.

How could I not have seen this coming? How could I imagine that the joy of connecting with my father would cancel out the inevitable feelings of loss? I think about calling someone but I can't imagine who, and besides, I don't know where these feelings will lead me and I don't have words for the terror of not knowing.

There is no way around grief, no waiting it out; it doesn't go away on its own, or with time. I know I have to travel into it, and the only way I know how to do that is through the art process. It is sorrow, finally, that leads me back to image making. Once again image making is not only something I long for, but something I desperately need. Art making holds and contains me in the raw material of my feelings in a way I have rarely risked with people. My anger toward the doctor only confirms my expectations, echoes old woundedness. I fear being misunderstood, misinterpreted, mistaken. I trust the art process. I have been frightened in its embrace, but never abandoned. Tools and materials stay reliably within their natures, never breaking promises, never betraying me. Yet I am in desperate need of human contact. Perhaps that is why, at this point, I want to make a mask, a remembrance of my father. The encounter with the doctor helps me see what I have been avoiding, what has pulled me off center. I can tolerate feeling exposed and vulnerable by holding the idea of making the mask. Art making gives me back a sense of purpose, replaces me in the flow of my life, signals the river.

At home I take out pictures of my father. Some are from when I was born: he's slim and happy with my aunts and uncles. Some are more recent: he looks bloated and tired. As he got closer to his death, he looked more like the younger pictures. I have made several of these masks before, the angry blue woman was one, and I have instructed clients in the process. There are many steps; it is a slow process and sometimes tedious. I need a slow process to keep me present in the feelings, otherwise I will surely flee back into busyness the minute the pain abates even a little. I take out a bowl for the base of the mask and some stiff gray Plasticene clay. I put the clay in an old pie tin and set it in the oven on low to soften. I have to work in the kitchen—it's too cold in my basement studio. Adina plays and gurgles in her high chair. The warmed clay, slightly greasy, feels good and forms easily over the bowl. This mask process, created by the artist Kari Hunt (Hunt and Carlson, 1961), involves making a mold and then using papier-mâché over it to form the mask. The first steps are especially slow, which is a good thing. I ease into a space where memories surface, feelings arise. My father clowns around in many of the pictures and almost always is touching or holding someone. I don't remember when we lost the ability to hug one another, but at some point were each too far into ourselves, too many false words had been spoken, to reach one another with even a gesture.

I turn away from the pictures to the job at hand. I manage to finish the rough, basic face shape before Adina gets cranky and wants to be fed. I am tired but grounded. We both fall asleep as I nurse her on the couch.

The next day I have to teach and don't get to the mask. When I return, I study the photos and gaze at the collected images of my father, including a stark pencil drawing I did during art school, full of dull pain and hatred. After my mother died, my father was mired in his own pain and numbed it with drinking. I drew him in a stupor in front of the television with a venom I didn't recognize at the time. At home on a school vacation, I recorded on paper what we all denied, that loss overshadowed our lives. How long ago did I lose my father? The drawing allows me to see feelings but is not at all sufficient to resolve them.

I begin to build up the features, and a face takes shape, his face. I am crying as I work, tears beading up on the oily surface of the Plasticene. Suddenly I am a baby, exploring his face with tiny fingers, he is dancing me around the kitchen and singing a silly, bouncy tune to make me laugh. It is a body memory of complete trust. I see him through infants' eyes and feel overwhelming love. Was he conscious of that? Did he ever know how unconditional, how total my love for him had been? I didn't know until I rediscovered it in that moment with my hands on the clay mask of his face. I look at Adina, and her face blossoms into a grin. I vow to stay mindful of the power of the love between us. I vow to remember how awesome is the trust that a child has in her parents.

Working in the clay absorbs me. I enter my feelings so intensely that past and present merge. I feel aching loss. No one I meet from now on will ever know him, Adina will never know him. I will never share any achievements with him. When I finished graduate school, he drove up with John for the ceremony. He stayed up past midnight in the lounge, talking and drinking with students, whose own parents slumbered sensibly in nearby hotels. I went to bed, glad my friends enjoyed his company but hoping he wouldn't be hungover and embarrass me the next day at graduation. He didn't.

I reexperience my love for him and my own feeling of being loved. All of this is evoked by working on the clay. I am centered in this experience by the mask forming under my hands, containing and honoring both the pain and the joy. Adina's presence and her needs anchor me in the present. She must be fed, changed, held. I am tired, broken open by today's work. But I've found the heart of gold in the grief. Touching early memories enlarges me and connects me to Adina as well as to myself. The river slows to a calm passage after much tumult.

Even when I can't get to the mask, knowing that it is in progress comforts me. I find myself thinking about it at odd times, when driving, and remembering more and more. In the following days the mask work seems a little easier. I spend a day refining the features, using my fingers, some clay tools, and even things from the kitchen drawers like a barbecue skewer. I prepare the materials to make the actual mask. I tear old newspaper into small pieces and put them into buckets of water, one for regular newsprint, one for Sunday comics. They must sit for a day or two in the water to soften the paper fibers. I love the simplicity of papier-mâché, the ordinariness of the materials, newsprint and wallpaper paste. My father read the newspaper every day. I do too, and now I think of him when I read, a small connection. This is not "fine" art, but art work.

Even the kitchen is chilly today as I sit down to layer the paper over the clay mask. The water in the buckets is icy, and I rinse my hands with warm water to keep going. First I layer on the plain newsprint, noticing that I have torn up the obituaries as well as the want ads. Then the soupy premixed wallpaper glue, then a layer of comics so I am sure I got a complete second layer. More glue and then the final layer of plain newsprint. The printed surface obscures any sense of a person. The mask looks too smooth; I want a more wrinkled, aged appearance. I experiment with rice paper, paper towels, and facial tissue to get the right effect. This is the face of his older years, not idealized. The eyes, inward, do not look at me. While he was dying, his gaze was so steady and clear, but many of my memories are of not being seen, as he looked inward into his own pain or beyond me to distraction. Now for drying, two or three days at least. I don't get back to the mask for a week.

Lifting the mask off the Plasticene is tricky. At this transitional stage the paper form is very fragile. I fear that it will not turn out, not be what I want, is really nothing at all. But I know this feeling will pass if I don't abandon the work. This is a moment for accepting imperfection; I want to get out of here fast. The urge to abandon the work rises up and then passes. But I must ease it up gently, taking care with the stuck places to avoid tears. Once off the clay, I hold the mask up to the light to look for weak spots. I remember my father's hands the summer before he died. He denied feeling poorly, but his hands felt like dried paper, with no strength, spotted with age. I make minor repairs and decide not to trim and finish the edge. The raw edge gives the image a feeling of emerging from a dream or fading into a mist. I paint on two coats of white gesso to prime the surface for painting. Now it is a ghostly death mask. Shadows in the darkening kitchen play over the contours of the features. I sit there until the sound of the garage door startles me. John comes into the kitchen and I shake myself back into the present. He admires the mask on his way through the kitchen. I can't begin to put all that it means into words.

More drying, more waiting. I welcome the workmanlike stages of mask making, I get some relief from the feelings and memories. Now I am intent on doing a good job and find it soothing to prepare the mask for the final stage of work. I've begun to feel energy returning in my life as well. Maybe I am finishing with the grief.

Finally, the mask is ready to be painted. Each stage has its own beginning and end, leading up to this final process. I set out my watercolors, a glass palette, a container of water, paper towels, and brushes. I hesitate, reluctant to finish, but the sensuous colors of the paint overcome my wish to avoid finishing. Painting the mask is a delicate process. I work for a while, then step away. The features look garish; almost any color is too much. I get a spray bottle of water from the ironing board, set up near the washing machine but rarely used. I spray a fine midst over the damp paint and watch as it runs down into the cracks and wrinkles, defining them. After much painting and unpainting the right amount of red tints the lips. Prus-

Fig. 17. Mask of My Father *(papier-mâché).*

sian blue and Payne's gray define the shadows. The art process is at work, healing me and taking over from any conscious thinking and judging. This absorption in the process is what heals, I am convinced. For a moment I forget the subject entirely; I am one with the river. I admire the mask dispassionately, as an artist, and am pleased. Then I look again, as a child who offers one last token of love and esteem, and I feel content that I have honored my father (fig. 17).

I feel renewed, refreshed. I think about art therapy presentations I might do on grief. I enter training to become a volunteer in the hospice program. My work there will serve as one of my internships for my doctoral work. I expect to work with the dying, but all the referrals I get are to work with children who have lost a parent.

When the grief resurfaces, I am caught off guard. It is June 1984, Father's Day. I am in a daze, unprepared for the impact this day has. John is out of town for the day. I am immersed in the feeling of meaninglessness that easily grays into wanting to die. I drag myself into the studio to draw. A warm-up drawing in red and gray is explosive, violent; the gray is calm but does little to dissipate the red. I try a scribble with my left, nondominant hand, hoping to outsmart my rational mind and get at the source of these feelings that have hit me like a sledgehammer. It is a sleeping angel. Another scribble, an angel with a baby. One more, a father angel welcoming a daughter. A welling up of feeling. That's it, die and join the father. He is so tender now, all the awful qualities gone. The person I loved so deeply is no longer hidden in so many layers of drink and deception, so blunted, so far away. He was returned to me for an instant. I want him back. I am exhausted and put the drawings away. The scribble drawing is good for searching, most effective when I am on the verge of feelings too hard to face. Place a piece of paper on a drawing board on the easel, close my eyes, let the pastel chalk meander in some overlapping lines. Then look into it for an image or a shape to coax into life. Then stand back and let the image speak.

Scribbles are for problem finding, but they don't solve anything, just point the way and sometimes unleash feeling. The next day I paint the scene again, more fully, in acrylic paint on board. I meditate on the picture of the father angel and daughter, allowing a dialogue to develop. The daughter no longer seems to have wings. The father is tenderly saying goodbye, comforting her but sending her back to life, her life. Dying, as my mother said, ain't as easy as it looks. But then, neither is living.

I am angry and depleted by this work. The demands of my outer life do not cease so that I can pursue the source of my grief. I know this is way back to balance, to the river. I know that the feelings will lodge in my muscles if they are not expressed, but I am tired. I use some clay to try and relieve the anger. As I work I am crying. It is God I am angry with. Why me? Why is grief the defining force of my life? When I look down, I have made a figure who crouches, beaten, looks up asking the question, Why me? The inside of the figure is gouged out, empty. I felt this way at fifteen, when my mother died. Why me? The figure is eyeless. I cannot see the meaning of pain.

I didn't share these drawings until writing this book. Unlike the mask, which has some finished, artistic qualities as well as being a container for emotion, the scribble drawings are raw. They are a direct conduit and they scared me. Was the doctor right, after all? Was I suicidal? Did I need medication, a hospital bed? If I had gotten those aids, would my grief have been lessened or just postponed? What if I had shown those drawings to someone, a therapist, even an art therapist? If that person hadn't known grief herself, would the images have helped me communicate or would they evoke fear? Is the art enough? It helped me release enough feeling that my life became more bearable, and the art pieces, especially the mask, let me share when I didn't have words. I feel empathy from others when they view the mask. The art allows me to own my feelings and eventually to see something universal in my experience. The scribble drawings show me how much I really lost and how deeply I mourn that loss, that I did, indeed, wish to be with my father. Suicide is the physical loss of self. It can parallel a symbolic loss of self.

I am astonished when I realize how much the art work took the place of people for me. When my father died, I didn't look to friends for support or share my sadness. I have shown the mask in several presentations on using art in the grieving process. This is very different from sharing one's pain when it is happening. Looking back, I can see that my method of coping was forged in my experience of my mother's illness and death. Our family believed in a kind of public stoicism that only rarely broke down, even in private.

Art making has many healing possibilities, the greatest of which is to allow relationship to develop. First, the relationship with one's self takes place in the making of the image. I felt my feelings when I made the mask of my father. That step made me more present in my feelings and able to accept comfort from those closest to me, my husband and sister. Sharing the art work in presentations allowed me to safely experience the empathy of others without being over-whelmed. One older woman asked me for the mask-making method after I spoke. She said she realized she had never grieved the sudden loss of her husband to a heart attack. She was thrust into the crisis of having to run his business immediately and had kept her feelings away for years.

The clay sculpture allowed me to see my vulnerability and slowly realize that needing others is how connections are made. The sculpture evoked the much deeper grief I felt and had never fully expressed over the loss of my mother. I still somehow thought that I must have done enough mourning, since her death occurred so long ago. Slowly, in the soul's own time, I was able to allow images of that most profound grief to emerge. Without making art I may never have learned at all how to allow others into my experience, how to feel a part of the human circle.

Ungrieved losses are sources of deep pain that etch patterns into our deepest self. These patterns are called forth and reverberate with any subsequent loss in our lives. Art making is a way of caring for loss. Therapists have long recognized the power of the anniversary of a loss to evoke feelings of grief still held within with an amazing freshness and primacy.

Grief is never entirely finished, though it may diminish and transform. To explore the meaning of losses in your life, first gather together photos or any other artifacts of the person. You may want to simply sit with them for a while or do some simple warm-up drawings. If the person whom you are grieving had some favorite music, play that while you work, if you can bear it. Your intention is to enter into the grieving process. You are likely to feel strong emotion, to cry and become sad. Be sure to undertake this work when you can allow some recovery time. You may become tired and require extra sleep. If you have had difficulty in letting yourself grieve or if the loss is one of long standing, consider planning to do these images on or near the anniversary of the loss or a birthday or other special time you shared with the person.

To create a mask, arrange your photos where you can see them easily while you cover a face-sized bowl first with plastic wrap, then with Plasticene clay. Plasticene is the oily kind of clay that you may have used in kindergarten. In art supply catalogues or stores it may be called sculptor's clay and is usually gray or green. If the clay is very stiff, warm it in a pie tin on the radiator or in the sun to soften it.

Gradually build up the features, using both your memory and your photo references. You can use clay tools, but your fingers and kitchen implements like barbecue skewers work just as well. Take your time. Part of the reason to do such an involved process as mask making is to dwell in your memories of the person. This will happen both consciously and unconsciously. If you begin to feel over-whelmed, let the mask sit for a while until you feel ready to return. Leave it where you will see it, and the process will continue inter-nally. Notice your memories and feelings as they rise and fall. Realize that your relation to this person continues within you and it always will.

When molding the features, it is helpful to exaggerate them somewhat because the application of papier-mâché will soften them. Once you have a complete image, apply a light coating of vegetable oil or petroleum jelly to aid later in the removal of the mask. Take two containers of water and add torn newsprint to one and torn comic pages to the other. Do not use the glossy pages; they don't adhere well. The mask requires three layers of paper. By using the black and white, then color, you can tell when you have completed each layer. Over each layer of paper, smooth a coating of wallpaper paste. You can buy either premixed or a powder type that you mix with water. Both are available in hardware stores.

Allow the mask to dry thoroughly before removing it from the mold. Any tears that result from removing the mask can be easily repaired with more paper and paste. Trim the edges and seal them

---

with a layer of paper and paste. Paint the mask inside and out with gesso or white house paint. The mold can be reused if you wish to have multiple images, or the clay can be re-formed into a new image.

You may wish to sit with the mask for a while before painting the features. Experiment freely with paint effects, remembering that you can always re-gesso and start again. If you intend to do a realistic face, you can mix a Caucasian flesh tone by using the primary colors, red, yellow, and blue with white. Start with a very small amount of each color with a larger amount of white. For skin tones in the olive range, use earth-tone versions of the primary colors: red oxide or Venetian red, yellow ocher, and a deeper blue such as Prussian blue. To get an African skin tone, experiment with greater amounts of red oxide and Prussian blue, or small amounts of premixed shade of violet. Experiment until you mix a pleasing shade. When finished, attach a string or wire to hang the mask. Fishline is strong and invisible for this purpose.

When your mask is done, spend some time contemplating your work. Notice your feelings and whether they have changed since you began. You may feel compelled to write about the person or to make additional images. Grief is deep water; one image can be helpful in wading in but will not make grief disappear. The mask may even seem to deepen your sorrow initially, particularly if you have never allowed your grief to surface before. Remember that sadness and tears are a way of honoring someone whom we love. Such feelings are a meaningful and necessary part of being human.

Consider how to witness your image. Friends or family members can join with you. Allow and expect that such an image, which you have put much into, will give comfort over time. Look around for the right place to display the image or, if that doesn't feel right, the right container in which to hold it. Consider creating your own ritual of honor by placing flowers, a candle, or incense before the image as an act of remembrance and respect on anniversaries or other important dates such as holidays.

Knowing the Past

Home from work, sick with the flu, unable to teach, having "lost my voice," I dream that my sister, my husband, and I are trying to straighten out some details about my father's estate. There is an I.O.U. that must be settled. At the same time, my father is back—still dead, but back in spirit. This means he is able to resume his previous physical form but he is quite childlike. In the dream I know that this condition occurs after death, where, for a brief period, he gets to come back and see the world as if for the first time but with understanding. He is very interested in the furnishings of my house, but not so interested in interacting with people.

We drive away to take care of this business matter in my sister's red station wagon. I am driving and I don't feel entirely in control; the car is too big and I am going a bit fast. We are traveling through farmland. Suddenly I realize the source of my unease. I left Adina with my dad. This realization is shocking. How could I have done this? He isn't capable of taking care of a baby in this child/spirit state he is in. Crying and feeling horrible, I turn back. The place we return to is my sister's house. People are out on the street, it's a warm summer evening, and the atmosphere is calm. I rush frantically into the house and find them in the basement. Dad is lying on his back, on the floor amid boxes and old furniture, hands folded, corpselike. Indeed, he has "died" again. The baby is at his head, on the floor, asleep and okay. My young nephew, Freddy, is sleeping next to the baby with his hand on her leg and has thus protected her from harm. I am relieved.

I draw the dream which seems to indicate a shifting from the "business of the outer world" to a focus on the cycle of relationships in the basement or unconscious. Parts of myself are coming into greater relationship: the old inner authority fades, while a new feminine consciousness and a new version of the inner masculine arise. I feel a deep longing for community, to be part of a group.

I work on a series of collages about my ancestors. Looking through pictures for the mask of my father, I come across some others that intrigue me, photos of myself as a child and some of my mother and uncles as children. I photocopy them so that I can cut and draw on the images with abandon. In one I stand, all in white, ready to make my First Communion. I combine that image with a pale angel on my left and a young tribal girl costumed for initiation on my right. Can the opposites be held? The angel looks worried.

I enshrine a photo of my mother as a toddler wedged between her Italian grandparents with labels from imported canned tomatoes (fig. 18). Food is one of my primary totems of the Italian side of my family. Both my parents were committed to seeing that no one ever left the table at our house hungry. Meals were a time of talk and laughter. One of my uncles was in the picture, behind my mother, his face swollen from a bee sting. I simply snip him out.

In another collage my father's father snores in a chair under the arc of a promise-filled rainbow formed by the colored stamps from my father's union dues book. The Statue of Liberty holds her torch aloft, calling others who, like my grandfather, flee famine or other hardships in their own country. I am the child of laborers, immigrants.

I place myself, at two or three, from a dreamy, out-of-focus snapshot, in a wondrous cave, gazing at stars. This image speaks to the sense of numinous wonder I lived in in my earliest memory. Me with three generations of the males in my family, daughter of the patriarchy. Images of American flags flanking us while behind us loom the sinister towers of industrialism, the dark side of the land of plenty, the price of the work that drew so many men to America.

These pieces bind me to my origins, child of immigrants who believed work would create a better life. Child of ritual, belief in

Fig. 18. Family Collage *(photocopied images and oil stick).*

God and country, in culture, in values and meaning. My ancestors left the countries in which they were born to travel to America. My journey is an inward one, from the ideas I was born into toward mysteries as yet unrevealed. Working with these images grounds me, reminds me of the wealth of my background. I am formed by those

I know and those I have only heard stories about. I feel my way into knowing about who came before me through the images.

I begin each collage by drawing energetically with large oil paint sticks, layer over layer of color. This ground of color creates an emotional space on which the images play. Laying down the ground, with some colors entirely obliterated, I sense the emotions and lives of individuals I will never know, yet whose character in some way I carry forth. These are real people who gave me life. Inner and outer life mesh, in the moment of working, and heal me. In moments like these I am often fooled into thinking I have it all figured out, that my life and my art will be smooth sailing from now on.

Many occasions can stir up the notion of exploring our past and family history. Weddings, funerals, births, religious life cycle events are often the catalyst. Many such events have been captured in photographs, which provide a starting point for image making. Family albums provide us with one version of our life. Working with these images can allow us to penetrate deeper into the story behind the story, another way to grapple with our personal myth, which has familial as well as cultural levels.

I particularly like photocopying original pictures because already one kind of transformation takes place. The usual color snapshot has been simplified into black and white. Using colored pencils or markers, I can re-create the images. I take away the Kodachrome of posed emotions and replace it with color of another key, more true to my experience.

Look through family albums for images that attract you. Make multiple copies of those. Consider enlarging and reducing some or photocopying fragments. Feel free to add copies of documents, maps, or newspaper or magazine images as a starting point. If my method appeals to you, use your oil pastels or get some oil paint sticks and create a ground of color on which to arrange your photo images. If you use oil paint sticks, use the heaviest paper you have or possibly gessoed cardboard. Consider the time frame of your photos,

What was the effect of world events on your family? What family stories are told about the past? Consider going to the library to get images of the time and circumstances you are working with. Sometimes the juxtaposition of a cultural or commercial image with the photos yields new interpretations or insights. We sometimes forget that our relatives lived in a different context that we do. Searching the photos for details that convey this is helpful. Noticing my grandfather's spittoon in one photograph brought back memories of his scent, tobacco and wool. Scent is a very powerful provocateur of emotion. If you know of a particular perfume or food or type of drink your relatives enjoyed, experiencing it can help you recall the past.

You contain all those who went before you. Using images in this way allows you to reweave the past and present and explore the multiple stories that are sometimes lost between the carefully posed pages of the family's official record. Ownership of your past enriches your life. Just notice what you've been given.

Part Five *Continuing*

Knowing Depth

I teach the active imagination process to my class. I decide to join them and make an image as well. My image is a seal, who seems wise and playful, basking on a rock in the ocean. In the visualization, the seal lumbers off and dives into the water. I expect it to swim toward a cave. Instead it swims up next to a huge rock, which rises up and turns. It is the back of the head of a huge creature. The head turns, the creature raises a hand. It is a beast/man or a man in a beast suit. He's silly-looking, and I am sick of him. He died and was transformed, wasn't he? What is he doing here now? His features seem so gross and exaggerated. Yet in subsequent days I try to remain faithful to the image process. I sculpt his unpleasant visage and make a papier-mâché mask. It seems to need to be worn. I attach elastic to the back and put it on, but halfheartedly. I have other work that draws me away from the river. I gladly leave him.

I have begun work on a Ph.D., partly to satisfy the requirements of keeping an academic job but more deeply because I feel pulled to understand the image process, to generate some "theory" to guide what otherwise often seems like random stabs in the dark with a paintbrush when trying to practice "art therapy." I am more and more uncomfortable with the marriage of art to psychotherapy as the basis of the work. Teaching is becoming excruciating; I feel I am in between voices. The relatively distant, professional role is no longer as comfortable as it once was. I find myself wishing to share my feelings about my images and about art therapy. I can't share my struggles with the students, whom I am expected to reassure. I don't think the few other professionals I know will understand. Art therapy is a relatively new field, and art therapists seem worried that unless we are uniformly cheerful and positive at all times, the field will simply disappear.

I'm back in the studio more regularly now while Adina sleeps or sits propped up in her baby seat, watching and playing with her toes. I do some scribbles, an elephant woman gazing at a shadow, a swan snake. Then I draw a tiny figure next to a pair of huge feet and legs. It is the image of a shamed child with downcast eyes next to a towering authority figure. How dare I question the wisdom of those who have come before me? The part of me who is the art therapy professor reminds me that if I choose this course of questioning, I will have to admit that *I* am not the towering authority figure, but rather the uncertain child. Can I give up this role I have worked so hard to achieve? What will the consequences be? And am I afraid to step on Margaret Naumburg's toes, as if, having initiated me into art therapy, she is still looking over my shoulder, disapproving of my direction. I recognize that I feel a little like a traitor in my Ph.D. work, trying to push away the Freudian psychology and the mechanics of psychotherapy while clinging to it at the same time. I try to reread Naumburg's books, which inspired me so many years ago, but they no longer hold my interest. I'm drawn away from them into the dark.

The next day I do a few warm-ups and get a massive, primitive woman from a scribble. I draw her in graphite, a huge body, tiny head, big hands and feet. She is sensation embodied. I draw her again, in color, sitting outside in some grass under a blue sky, closer to the realm of sensation. But she demands clay, to be sculpted from the earth. I get some red clay and form her contours. Very little indication of face, barely a mouth. She is the feminine as mountain, rooted in the earth, peaceful. I make a little platform for her, covered in purple cloth with a structure of tree bark. I want to honor this aspect of the feminine. I am making an altar, I realize, and that makes me nervous. I lay some objects on the platform with the sculpture, a leaf, a stone, a pine cone, a shell, attributes of this earth goddess (fig. 19). I remember reading about household goddesses, which were prevalent before the rise of monotheism, worshiped in an everyday

Fig. 19. Preserver Altar *(clay, wood, mixed media).*

way, not in temples or churches. I feel I am doing something faintly sacrilegious but compelling at the same time.

I am curious also about the need to sculpt. That important images surface three-dimensionally interests me. Is it my lack of training in sculpture that leaves an open door? Sculpture, more than any art process I use, makes things real, alive. I can't choose *only* to sculpt. The image decides what it needs to be made of. The direct use of my hands on the clay, with no paintbrush or pencil as intermediary, heightens the experience of receiving an image, as one might receive an infant in a birth. The lack of trained skill forces me to rely on intuition and sensation, how the clay feels in my hands.

In June, Adina is a year old. I want to explore the theme of mother and child. I begin with a few scribbles, energetic and benign. I keep thinking somehow the art process is all going to order itself in my life one day and become neat. I will wake up one morning and know I am a painter, who paints mother and children, for example. I wish for an orderliness that doesn't occur. This river meanders and goes where it wants, taking me with it. A winged figure emerges from one of the scribbles, surveying the earth from above. Then, a horrible red mother and child. The mouths seem to have a life of their own. The mother's eyes are crazed; will she eat the child? Is the child part of the breast? (fig. 20). Feelings of lust, merger, wanton abandon. Here she is, fire hair turning into snakes, the other side of the quiet, cowlike figure who rests on the purple platform. Is the generativity of the Earth Mother only possible if her opposite—the voracious, dangerous, destructive aspect—is recognized? How easily I project that part onto others.

I look around the studio and all I see are mouths, in masks, in drawings, in the red baby sculpture. Adina is so "mouthy" right now, sucking, eating, screaming. My urge is to feed her whenever she screams; I want to be the "good mother," but at times she is only asserting herself. I need to feed my own internal baby who is screaming in rage to be heard, kicking her legs and flailing her arms. I feel ripped apart by this real baby and by the imaginal one, and now by this devouring mother. I sculpt a plaque of a tiny smiling angel baby with gold wings to temper my rage with humor and to allay my fear of unleashing destruction (fig. 21).

What is destruction anyway? Where is its place in art and in life? Psychology calls this the "bad mother," hypothesizing that the infant splits its knowledge of the nurturing person in two: the "good" one who feeds and takes care, the "bad" one who neglects or devours. I project the bad mother onto other women; that preserves my own goodness. Drawings come from these thoughts. On a five-foot-long piece of mural paper is the bad mother. Medusa-like, she has snakes for hair, a green face, and haggard, tired eyes with red irises. She has blue, cold hands and dangerous nails, holding a baby at empty breasts. Any mother is the bad mother if she is tired enough. Isn't this allowed? She fades into nothingness, no lower body, no blood, no sex. Her mouth reveals a void. She is a frightening vision of the mother as unfed, the empty trying to give. I shun her and turn to

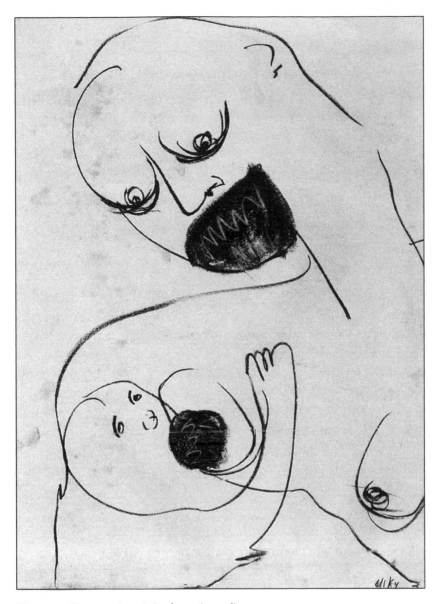

Fig. 20. Devouring Mother *(pastel).*

her opposite, the good mother, strong and earthy, moon-faced and round. She is simple but sturdy, my enculturated fantasy, the woman as ever-giving breast. Both of these alternatives are extreme. To be all-giving is to be mindless of one's own needs, but to give mindfully

Fig. 21. Angel Plaque *(painted clay).*

means recognizing fatigue, depletion, my own limits. I am not good at this. I give to my family, my students, my clients, but I am less able to receive.

How to explore this paradox of the feminine? It feels dangerous and spills over into my life. I struggle with women in authority; I see them as having dark and hidden motives to undo me. I contain my feelings about women in my present life in a piece about Naumburg. Safely dead, she serves to carry all the dark burden of the jealous, bad mother that I see in older professional colleagues. I try to maintain an open, giving state with students, clients, coworkers. I know the shadow is mine, yet I can't own it. I see others as taking, and I don't know how to set limits. My image of myself as a woman is incomplete and organized around giving and doing. I realize my internal feminine self doesn't really have a voice at all.

I am moved to make a large piece, different from any I have done before. It is a large garment of rough linen, fringed with unwashed sheep's wool. I found the fabric stuffed in a closet in the basement of the house we live in. The sheep's wool is matted and greasy and smells of animals. I create a necklace of bones and singing heads to hang around the neck. A stole depicts the phases of the moon. A mask of the sun tops the piece. This is Death's Vestment (fig. 22), another side to the life-death quandary I have been stuck in, the singing over the bones, from death to life. I am reminded that in the world of plants and animals, death is not a catastrophe, but a seasonal, cyclical occurrence. How is it we have forgotten so much? I like this piece and hang it in a stairway in our house. The piece seems to complete my grief, something I am always hoping will occur.

An image comes of myself picking a pear from a tree. The image reassures me that I am right to seek to bring all this messy stuff to consciousness. Evoking Eve taking the apple from the tree of knowledge, I feel confirmed yet uneasy. Life for Eve became more complicated after she gained knowledge. I don't trust the traditional patriarchal version of her story, but what will my version be?

Looking back, I marvel that the images contained all that was happening as well as they did. My own motherhood opened the door to an onslaught of images. I was being challenged by these images as I was externally being challenged by circumstances. If my baby-sitter was sick on a day I had to teach, and John could not be home, I brought Adina and laid her down for a nap on a pile of students' coats in our classroom. If I had to attend a meeting, I brought her and nursed her, which the other faculty professed not to mind. I was involved in maintaining my public image and fulfilling my duties as wife, mother, teacher, and therapist. Generally I pretended it was no problem to do this. In reality, it required enormous

Fig. 22. Death's Vestment *(papier-mâché mask, fabric, bone)*.

energy. I was also still somewhat frightened of the power of the images and worried that, if given free reign, they would topple my carefully planned life. Which is eventually exactly what they did.

The archetypes don't come all at once. They dance us back and forth across the line between the personal and metaphysical. They arrive again and again, in different garb, more clearly in focus, more powerfully present. For me, the mother archetype has been enormously powerful in my life. Is it because my actual mother died, leaving a hole in me through which the archetypal forces flow unchecked? Is it also partly because we live in a time when feminine roles are up for examination and changes in what it means to be a woman are rampant?

What is your guiding image? What image most intrigues you or seems to surface again and again in your dreams and imagination and artwork? Pay attention to it; the guiding image returns to deepen your understanding, to enlarge your possibilities. Welcome it and what it comes to teach you. Notice if a particular person in your life seems to represent an aspect of your compelling archetype. It could be a mentor, a lover, a coworker, or even someone outside your direct experience. Cultural icons like movie actors or performers become important to large numbers of people partly because they present an opportunity for us to project our archetypal needs onto them.

Create an image of yourself in relation to such a person. By investing this person with archetypal significance, what role are you symbolically choosing for yourself? If your lover is the hero, are you playing the role of damsel in distress? My investment in Margaret Naumburg as a powerful mother figure relegated me to the role of shamed child when I began to challenge her ideas professionally. This occurred partly because I had no experience struggling for independence from an actual mother. Working in the realm of the image helped me to claim the power of authority for myself and proceed with original doctoral work rather than remaining in a daughter role and simply restating Naumburg's ideas.

Working with images does not preclude the need to have actual relationships in order to grow and change. It does, however, help us be more conscious and learn the lesson inherent in any challenging relationship rather than staying stuck in repetitive patterns. Challenges come to help complete us. Notice how doing the image work affects your challenging relationships.

Remember that image work is powerful. If you choose to explore a problematic current relationship, be sure to do so safely.

Make sure to state your intention clearly, to come to greater understanding and comfort in your relationships, to be more aware of the roles your choose to play. Keep your work private and choose any witness carefully. Through images you can come to understand your options and discover solutions.

You may need to vent some strong feelings, which the image will reliably contain. Go at a comfortable pace. A mistake that is sometimes made is to assume that once you have reached an understanding, simply sharing it will heal a relationship. Remember that the image work is yours. The object of your image will not necessarily receive and respect your work, see the light, and change.

If you do decide to share such work, be sure to ask yourself: What is my intention? Discuss your plan with a trusted witness and share the work first with someone who can be reliably supportive. Know your desired outcome and then let it go. When you have reached a sense of peace with your image and are mindful of your motives, if it feels right, then share it.

9

Knowing Fear

I am walking down the street past a little cobblestone alley blocked off by black wrought-iron gates that are locked at night to prevent cars from driving through for a shortcut. With a start I "see" the image of a black dog locked behind the gates. The dog behind the gates came in a dream the night before—I had forgotten all about it. When I get home, I draw the dog, sharp yellow teeth and yellow eyes glinting in a large head. This dog is huge and full of energy, wolflike.

I craft a mask of this creature, building with plaster gauze over a cardboard and newspaper armature. The plaster soaks through the cardboard and paper, all but dissolving it. The piece becomes heavy and unwieldy at this stage, but I use these materials because I want it to be substantial, which the plaster is, once it dries. So I work slowly and prop the piece up with coffee cans so it doesn't collapse. The drying process is interminable, as the wadded-up newspaper I use to form the jaws pulled back over snarling teeth soaks up the water in the plaster and then has to dry from the inside out. Finally the dog is dry enough to paint. The bars in the dream do not appear in the drawing, nor are they a part of the mask piece (fig. 23). Making the image frees the dog, who seems like a guide, another variation of the dark beast who appears at times of transformation.

Over time the dog chases me, biting at my heels to keep me moving along the path in the dark. I create another sculpture, a full-scale dog, by building an armature of chicken wire and covering it with strips of cloth and glue (fig. 24). The dog is black and red, with teeth that glow in the dark, painted with phosphorescent paint.

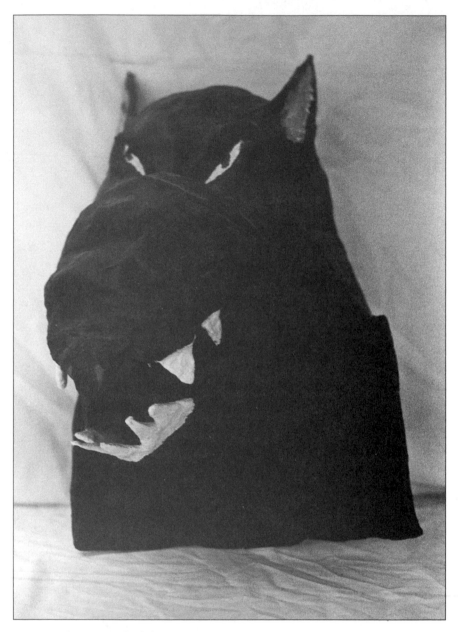

Fig. 23. Dog Mask *(plaster gauze).*

Fig. 24. Dog Sculpture *(canvas over chicken wire, acrylic paint).*

In a bookstore, while I'm browsing with no intention to buy, a thin volume about Kali falls off the shelf. She is the feminine aspect of the dark third of the Hindu divine triad of Creator-Preserver-Destroyer. I have sculpted the Preserver, the solid earthy goddess, but who is Kali? As I read about her, I realize I have seen only her psychologized aspect of the feminine, the mother who is depleted from giving. Nothing a good vacation wouldn't cure. In Hindu mythology she is much more potent. She eats the children to whom she gives birth, she holds the bloody dismembered head of her consort while they embrace, she wears a necklace and skirt of skulls. Her images fascinate me, as there seems to be no equivalent in the Judeo-Christian iconography. She is revered in Hinduism as the aspect of creation that takes back, eventually, all that is created; she is not some split-off "bad" mother. In our sanitized culture we reject death and decay and hide the parts of life that Kali represents.

I make a drawing of her (fig. 25) and then a painting. I feel electrified by these pieces. She is fierce and full of energy, using her weapons to cut through artifice and lies. She effects the necessary destruction of the old, not calmly but powerfully. I find her energy exhilarating. Out running one morning shortly after making the Kali painting, I encounter a huge black dog running free, unusual in my neat suburban neighborhood. I stop in my tracks and stare at the dog. It stares back and then trots away.

At this point my academic career is crumbling and I feel Kali's sword, the curved harpe that is used to cut down wheat. I am destroyed and I am afraid. I make a painting in which a woman rails against her fate while a black dog howls the moon in the background. My vision of myself is annihilated. The two towers began as the stark concrete high-rise buildings on the campus where I teach. I have been told that I will not be recommended for tenure, that while I have done a great deal, and very well at that, it is not enough.

I fight the decision, and it is overturned in an interesting way: I am offered several more years to keep trying to meet unrealistic expectations. In the meantime, I learn the decision has much more to do with internal department politics than anything I may have

Fig. 25. Kali *(pastel).*

done or could ever do. Feeling as though I am working in an environment slightly more demented than what Alice found after following the white rabbit down his hole, I respectfully decline the offer.

Still reeling, I take a job in an art school teaching art therapy part

Fig. 26. Kali Altar *(mixed media).*

time, hoping and expecting it to be different. In one of my classes, while students create their own totem sculptures, I make a small, many-armed figure of Kali. At home I set up a small altar to her in my studio (fig. 26), to allow this energy its due while I mourn my career and my self-image, once again in shambles. I light red candles to the Destroyer and pray for the grace to let go of what no longer serves me.

I am depressed and physically depleted after the unpleasant battle with my previous university job over tenure expectations. I ache all over and decide to seek some bodywork to find myself again. What I find amid the grief over losing my job is myself mourning my mother, something I thought I had finished long ago.

I have a pounding headache that will not abate. In active imagination I see an image of my mother in my head, trying to get out. I visualize her floating upward, out of my aching skull. Is it possible that my grieving, my wanting to hold on to her, keeps her soul from rest? Is it only her, or is it also the wish for the all-good, only-good mother I am mourning? I never thought of grief that way. I draw her leaving my head and then decide to make a mask of her, similar to the one I made of my father, in the hope of releasing both of us from bondage. I gather pictures of her. There aren't so many; she was more often the one taking the photos rather than being in them. I find a few that show her with dark, sad eyes set in a dark face. I try to sculpt her features in the warmed Plasticene clay to form the mold for the mask. This sculpting process was so satisfying and immediate when I did the piece for my father. I expect to evoke long-forgotten memories and perhaps meet my mother and reconnect to early good feelings. Most of my conscious memories are of her as a very sick person battling cancer.

Instead, the clay will do nothing. The features, except for the nose, refuse to form. After working for an hour or so, I am frustrated and slash off the misshapen face in despair. I fear the image process has betrayed me. I know I have to wait to find the answer, and I go off to other things. When I return to the face, I let my hands take over, relinquish my expectation and wishes for a certain outcome. Some of the slash marks make interesting furrows down what should be the cheeks. I begin to follow these with my fingers until a form emerges. No eyes, no mouth. This is a mask of pain, of tears unshed, in a face hardened into stone by a relentless holding back of feeling. Tears begin to stream down my own face. This is the inner face of my stoic, saintly mother. The price of tears uncried that have cut right through to the bone (fig. 27). This face is the price of not finding the river, not yielding to its twists and turns. Not crying out in anger and fear for a lifetime. Kali triumphs. In my logical attempt to make a mask the way I have before, I cannot find the way. It is in the destruction of the piece that I find the true mask.

No warm memories—instead I have excavated a pain-filled si-

Fig. 27. Mask of My Mother *(papier-mâché).*

lence. My mother and generations of women before her suffered in silence. This is my legacy. I remember the bone face mask that seemed so primitive, as if feeling were an undeveloped function for me. I have some idea now why that is so. I recall another mask I made a few years before. At the time I thought it frivolous. It is a nice lady with two Band-Aids crisscrossed strategically over her mouth, lest something inappropriate slip out and ruin her facade. She is my compromise with Kali, the silencing of feeling, the denial of my own sword, my ability to seek and speak the truth. I am the lady with Band-Aids when I handle everything without complaint. I find anger rising up. I will break the silence.

This is not an easy, happy task. I cast a mask of my own face, mouth open, screaming. I picture it in a wooden box, held, bound. I find on old wooden box, which I paint black and red. I sit with the mask a long time, years. Then one day I realize I have to break the box. I take a hammer and smash it. The broken glass that years ago I felt was inside me, that I tried so carefully to avoid feeling, now spews forth from the mouth and eyes of the mask, housed in the broken box (fig. 28). The confining box of existence is broken by the expression of pain. The river proceeds. The black dog has delivered me into a hard place.

I had no image to express feelings of rage and pain. Angry women are crazy women, out-of-control women. The most potent image in my repertoire is the crucifixion, which expresses pain and torment but in a context of passivity, acceptance, and sacrifice. Kali is different: she expresses an active aspect of destruction. I resisted as long as I could, seeing that my well-crafted professional life was stagnant. I tried to tinker and change it in small ways. In giving up my university position, I gave up much more than a job. I began to give up an image of myself as able to do it all, a variation on Superwoman.

The crucial element in making the change was deep longing for my creative self. I had to face the fact that the requirements of keeping an academic job, even in an art therapy department, have little to do with exercising one's creativity. I was not able to fit image making into a neat schedule between lectures, publishing, and research and baby feedings and making dinner on the checklist of a neat modern life. So the river that nourishes the soul rises up and wreaks havoc—out of love for us, I believe. It is hard to believe when one thing is taken from us that something else is being given. Trusting in the infinite love of the soul takes practice.

In making the Kali images, I felt the weight of generations of women who obediently, obsequiously, did the right thing and kept quiet about their own needs and desires, who answered the needs of parents and husbands and children but not necessarily of their own souls. I prize the Kali image, the lesson that the letting go of what doesn't work and what is stale and old in my life is a form of neces-

Fig. 28. Shattered *(paster gauze, wood, glass fragments).*

sary violence. I keep her altar in my studio, with dried seeds, dead flowers, and red candles, which I light when I realize I want to let go of something in my life.

As powerful as Kali's appearance in my life was, I did not submit to her wisdom easily or all at once. I took another job right away, which let me hang on to my self-image, and some of the same issues eventually surfaced again. Change, like any other dying, is harder than it looks.

Embracing the image process can bring up fears. Yet entering into our worst fears, paradoxically, is the path of renewal. Kali came into my life as an image of the active nature of destruction or change. I offer her as representing an aspect of life that we often seem to deny. She is present in earthquakes, fire, storms. She is present in the events in our lives that seem cataclysmic.

Ask yourself what you fear. If you initially come up with fairly general answers, try to trace them back to specifics. What are you hanging on to for fear of letting go? If Kali were to enter your dreams with her sword, what would she cut out of your life? What is old, stale, blocking your growth and renewal?

Kali is a powerful meditation. If you choose to ask her help, you are inviting a powerful archetypal force to aid you. This force acts in our lives anyway, but asking can help us be conscious of and work with this force. State your intention. What area of your life needs renewal? You need not be specific in naming what might come into your life. We don't usually know what should replace the old, which is part of the reason we cling to the old—at least it is familiar. Focus your intention by creating an image. Honor your resistance. Consider using a scribble or wet-into-wet painting as a starting point. What does it suggest to you? Take your time to discover what emerges. We cannot know the nature of transformation beforehand.

Consider creating an image of Kali to aid you in understanding what needs to be given up. Remember that destruction is a vital and necessary part of the creative cycle. You can state your intention in small ways as practice, too. Clean out a closet, get rid of old clothes or books or something symbolic of an old relationship, role, or job. These are ways of signaling your willingness to move through fear to change.

Knowing Projection

I facilitate an art therapy supervision seminar in my new job. Students bring in artwork done by clients and talk about the work they are doing. The students are an interesting group, more diverse than the students I taught at a state university. One student, however, gets on my nerves. I hear my voice, sharper than it needs to be, cutting her off, too often, in midsentence. There is much to admire about her: older than most graduate students, she balances schoolwork with the demands of a husband and children. But I don't feel admiration. Something annoys me, beyond the realm of reason. She also annoys other students, who indicate at times that they consider her "just a housewife." She works with children in a private school and takes every word uttered by her supervisor there, a self-important psychologist, as gospel. Where is her critical thinking? Her girlish appearance, quickness to shed tears, and wide-eyed, earnest attempts to take in my criticism are driving me mad. The more I try to control my remarks, the more I seem driven to tirade.

What bothers me most is her ill-fitting use of psychological theories to explain the art of the children. Using the words of theorists who work with seriously disturbed children to describe the art of normal kids in a private school infuriates me. She is unable to just *see* what the child draws as a statement of the child's interest and inner world to be appreciated for itself. Instead, the boy who draws lots of trees is "obsessive"; the girl who enjoys drawing shapes and filling them in with colors is "compulsive." I have to remind myself that applying these clinical terms too freely is a forgivable blunder for art therapy graduate students, not something worthy of censure.

Later, at home, I decide to draw a picture. I want to see what the image would reveal, not so much about the student as about me. Can I find the source of my negative feelings? What is my image of her? I sit down with a sheet of paper and some well-sharpened colored pencils, a medium of precision and control, qualities I find lacking in this student's work. Get quiet, focus on her in my mind's eye, feel that tensing of my shoulders as I wince at her description of a child's painting, the vague, halting presentation, peppered with twenty-five-cent words, used ineptly. I draw the figure first. She's chasing balloons. I draw her floating in space, reaching up for the bright balloons of "knowledge," colorful and attractive to her, important words from textbooks, her supervisor, me. Her hair is flowing, her form amorphous and unclothed, childlike and vulnerable. Yes, that's her all right, a hapless pixie, trying to grasp so much hot air.

I find myself drawing a ground line and filling it in with green and brown strokes. As I look at the image, I feel better. The figure looks as much like me as like the student. The face is open, seeking—that is true of her, though I've been blind to that aspect in class. The key, though, is her feet, floating above the ground line. That's it. She isn't grounded. When she gets hold of a balloon, it just carries her away into foolishness, up into the thin air of theory, too far away from the ground of common sense. Her essential problem is that she doesn't value her own perceptions. Assuming she knows less, she dutifully accepts the words of the "experts," myself included. That and her desire to be a good girl. She simply honors the implicit contract of graduate school, conscientiously, if uncritically, carrying out of the role of student.

But this still doesn't explain why she gets on my nerves so. What does she mirror back to me that I find uncomfortable? Over the years in working as a therapist I have come to value common sense over theories. Yet if common sense is all there is to it, how do I justify teaching in a graduate program? Here's a woman paying a lot of money to be told that all this studying is causing her to lose the basic knowledge she came into the program with, a poor exchange indeed. Her openness is a hazard. Fine. But why does this rile me so? *I* often feel that art therapy is only colored balloons, attractive but ephemeral, a needless manipulation of the basic human urge to make images. I even feel sometimes that what art therapists do is an assault to the soul. If I see what I am teaching as so much hot air, that threatens my status as an expert, my job as an educator. Worst of all, she is a woman trying to do it all, take care of her family and have a career—and she complains about it out loud. I still don't want to admit there is anything hard in this.

I shift my focus from the student to myself. I want to bargain with Kali. Do I have to quit teaching entirely to get my own feet back on the ground? This is a scary proposition. I like being associated with a prestigious institution. I have my own fears of feeling like "just a housewife" if I can no longer say I teach at this or that university. Can't I just think this one out? Do I really have to change my life? Isn't insight enough?

The incident I have just described is significant because it involves an unequal relationship in which, as the teacher, I had more power. Struggling to understand our part in such relationships is an especially important responsibility. Children, students, and subordinates pull on particular parts of us, those relegated to what Jung called the shadow. People in subordinate positions cannot always easily discern when we are reacting to them out of our own denied struggles. For this reason, it is crucial to look at what therapists call "countertransference," or the unconscious feelings that determine our behavior in such relationships.

People to whom we react strongly are often a source of powerful images for us. This is particularly so when we react to them with unreasonable negativity, although there are also times when we idolize someone who manifests positive traits we are unable to acknowledge in ourselves. Irritation or idealization, like the grain of sand in the oyster, can give rise to the pearl of wisdom. Rather than trying to control people and determine the outcome you unconsciously need, consider that they are teachers for you. Identify a person in your life whom you have unreasonably overvalued or unfairly persecuted. If you are a parent, doing this exercise about a child is very useful. Otherwise, any student or person in a subordinate position is fine. Spend a few moments dwelling on his or her qualities and behavior. Do a drawing; it can be very simple. Exaggerate the annoying or wonderful attributes—you really want to get at the heart of the matter. Consider the image for a moment as a self-portrait. What is this person mirroring to you? What is he or she holding that for whatever reason you are unable to bear in your own awareness? What is there for you to learn? What arises in response? Are there memories or feelings? How is the situation with this person like one you experienced in the past when you were the less powerful partner? Just notice what comes up. Journaling can help you follow the threads of memories.

You may find your irritation or idealization shift or disappear once you place the conflict into the realm of the image. This frees you to relate to the person in simpler and less charged terms. Most important, it lets you know what qualities in yourself require your attention.

Parents in particular place a great burden on children by unconsciously shifting unacceptable aspects of self onto the child. This is equally true if the shift involves a positive trait: for example, the parent who idealizes a child's athletic or musical ability and requires the child to invest enormous time in perfecting a skill that the parent never acquired. Obviously this is quite different from honest support of a child's achievement. There is a distorting effect that occurs because the achievement does not feel genuine to the child and the work to achieve it is onerous rather than enjoyable. It takes considerable awareness and courage to see this dynamic, but the image will help.

By viewing the image as a self-portrait, you may recognize unrealized dreams that may still be within your reach in some form. If you pursue them yourself, your child or student will be freer to become an authentic person and not an auxiliary to your own needs.

This task can be used anytime you find yourself struggling in relationship with a child, spouse, friend, or coworker where there is a built-in imbalance of power. The clarification of the image sorts out personal material from actual disagreements and actually defuses the emotional nature of many struggles. Although the intention here is to learn more about oneself, growing in compassion for others is a common by-product. This is another task where sharing the image should be done with care, probably best with a neutral and caring person not directly involved in the struggle.

Knowing the Unknown

I am receiving bodywork in 1988, trying to undo the armor my muscles have formed in the months following my transition to the new teaching job. With careful work, I begin to relax, and the pain of the present struggle mingles with past hurts and comes flowing outward. The image of a tiny dead bird comes to me during one of these sessions. I sketch it in my journal when I return home.

I decide to write a book about art therapy; this and not teaching, I tell myself, is my "real" job. But I am intensely frustrated: the writing is academic and boring, the years in academia have left their imprint. I go for a walk to clear my head. I come across a dead baby bird on the sidewalk on my path. Instantly, I return in memory to age three or four, before school age. I am crouching down on my heels in the alley next to my house. There lies a baby bird, pale beak, bulge of unopened eye, nearly imperceptible blue veins beneath translucent skin. It is cool and dark in the shadowed alley between the two houses. I leave the alley after a while to resume playing in the sun, but I come back throughout the day to check on the tiny creature. Ants are eating it; by the end of the day it is gone without a trace. My first awareness of death: mystery at three, mystery still.

I go home and get my camera and return to take some black and white pictures of the bird and then lay it carefully in the grass under a nearby tree. This image feels like a totem, first appearing in my vision, then showing up on the street and carrying me back in time to my earliest memories. I develop the photos and frame a tiny one in a flowered pewter frame and put it on the desk where I write (fig. 29).

Fig. 29. Bird *(photograph).*

The bird continues to haunt me, returning me to memories of a time that are mostly shadow, soft and vague but also magical. This is the time I tried to capture in the collage of myself in the blue cave gazing up at stars, a magical interlude when time was seamless, my childhood before the storms of illness overtook my family. If I try to focus and search my mind, the memories disperse like fog. Something numinous is there that resists my efforts at understanding.

I want this bird to wake up and fly away, be a sturdy little survivor. But it is mute and gray. I have a bird's nest in the studio that I found somewhere, and I photograph it in a tree branch and then in my husband's hands. I sandwich the two negatives together and make a print of the bird in the nest. It is ghostly, like a watery reflection. I think of the nest that the bird fell from, blind to the fact that my daughter is starting first grade this year, going to school all day, needing me less. Blind to my unwillingness to allow the death of my work as a teacher of art therapy.

John and I are also struggling with the decision about whether or not to have another child. I have a dream:

> I am sitting on the floor thinking about having another baby. I don't want to be pregnant again. Then I see that there is a baby on the couch and she is my baby. What am I supposed to do with her? Put her up for adoption? I have to deal with *this* baby. I am somewhat annoyed that she exists, getting in the way of my plans. I pick her up; she rears back and won't let me hold her. The baby says, "You are not the mother." She is having an allergic reaction to me, getting red and blotchy all over. I pick her up and call the doctor. The baby's head is wounded. My aunt points out that there is a shunt in the back of the baby's head. I am alarmed. I didn't even know I had this baby or anything about her problems.

I draw the dream and realize it is time to disengage from the mother archetype. Its time to get back to that wounded baby who died early on, my baby, me. Somehow it seems easier, more acceptable, to have another baby than to commit my time to my own creative work. I feel confident about having a baby, I know what to do; my own work will put me on the edge, and that feels much riskier.

In my teaching too, even depressed and tired, I feel I know what I am doing. My students appreciate my teaching, and I want to continue. The alternatives—quitting and really getting immersed in my own writing and art—should be thrilling, but they aren't. I am afraid I will disappear. Without a job, a title, holding a child's hand, who am I? Who is just me? I still haven't answered that question.

It is always hard for me to accept how far the distance is between having an "insight" into my life and actually having life change. I'd known for years that I wasn't entirely clear about who "I" was. I understood how the role I played in my family trained me to focus on others, to meet their needs and remain unmindful of my own. I knew that the challenge of becoming more fully myself lay in my creative work. Yet the gratification of doing things that fit with my early roles, being a wife, a mother, a therapist, a teacher, were also real. Abandoning those roles was not my answer. I needed the firm ground of my family and their love and support while I faced my internal struggles. I was surprised when I made the photograph of the empty nest to discover how deeply I had buried myself in filling my daughter's needs, as if I could undo through her what I had missed. I often collaborated with her on artwork for hours rather than make time for work that was strictly my own. I vicariously enjoyed the adulation she received. I wanted the unconditional acceptance a child is accorded, not the critical regard offered to an adult. I didn't know how to get that just for myself, yet as an art therapist that is exactly what I so often provided for others.

The little dead bird activated my compassion for the little girl I had been, pulled away too soon from childhood. I needed to nurture the part of me that needs uncritical love in order to be able to tolerate the risk of growing and changing through a critical view. The fear of criticism and rejection has been a force that has prevented me from sharing my images more freely and paradoxically from gaining the loving witness I also need.

The hardest thing to realize is that I can't fix it all and then begin to share, that fixing it isn't the point at all. The point is being in the river and enjoying all the twists and turns, the rough parts and the calm.

How does one go back to unfinished places in the soul? I had lived the mother for so long, in so many guises; how to be the child? The answer for me resides in art making and play. Besides the dominant archetype, each of us also has, lurking in the shadows, shunned images who have unlived potential. Who is your shunned image? Whom have you exiled from your soul? What potential have you neglected? Is there an image in you that was thwarted early on that can now be reclaimed?

One way to think about this is to recall things from childhood, favorite activities, places, foods, toys, or clothes. These can touch off memory and bring back images. What were your dreams and wishes at five, at seven? Ballerina, cowboy, truck driver, wolf? Draw these images and welcome them into your life like the long-lost orphans they are. Make a story box to house your childhood dream. Don't worry if the images seem childish. Don't try to dress them up or make them perfect. Remember they are undeveloped and like a little sprout caught under a rock, need your assistance to grow and flourish.

Reaffirm your intention to accept and honor these parts of yourself. Play with them like old friends. Then notice if any ideas surface of things you might do to nurture this unlived potential. Maybe you can take a dance class, learn to ride a horse, or set aside time to hike through the woods. These are the openings to knowing the roots of your creative self. Hang up your images, live with them, and let them guide you.

Knowing Collaboration

She is a wild woman astride a laughing snake. She surfaced in a sketch I did in a workshop on the Goddess years ago, and I put the image up, though thinking it a little weird. Then I find two sticks that evoke the same image, this tall, stringy form astride a snake that acts as a balance. They stay that way, just two sticks, for a long time, but I never throw them away or use the sticks for anything else. Finally, for some reason, I begin to work on her, whittling the snake stick so that it tapers at the end, carving out a dented place to form the snake's laughing mouth. I paint the woman figure a soft pink and build her some breasts out of wood putty. She stays armless for a while. Unraveled nylon rope, spray-painted gold, becomes her electric hair. Twigs serve as her arms, and a knot in the wood is a fox peering out from between her legs (fig. 30).

The feminine force of creativity is wild and unpredictable, charged with energy. This is a piece of the feminine I have often confused with craziness and mental illness and tried to keep under wraps. She may be more foreign to me than even Kali, the Destroyer.

Creator-Preserver-Destroyer, three aspects of the feminine, finally all represented in images to guide me. I light candles to all three, but I am intimidated most by the Creatrix. Her chaotic, enveloping energy strikes on its own schedule, hauling me out of bed in the middle of the night, without regard to my other duties. She scares me. What will people say? What will my family say when I decide I have to sleep out on the deck under the full moon? What will guests think when they see these strange little figures, with

Fig. 30. Creatrix *(painted wood, found materials).*

dishes of ash in front of them? I decide not to care. The Creatrix is the catalyst and inspiration, the bright flame and wild dance. She works in strange ways. I wonder if I have the courage to trust her.

She calls me to return to the three masonite panels abandoned five years before. Now I recognize the lizard-headed woman. She is the feminine force. Now I can paint in the male faces in each painting because I am not fighting her, closing my eyes to her quite as much. In the first painting, She is approached by a man, a coarse, pompous man in a top hat and cloak. His relationship to the feminine is voyeuristic. He crouches behind the stairs, watching her like a theatergoer spying on the leading lady. What was once a rose on the staircase that separates them becomes a candle. She offers him illumination, knowledge.

In the second panel, they stand before an unseen altar in marriage. He has changed: his face becomes cartoonish, and he is attended by a young boy. On either side behind them are arrayed their constituents. His is represented by the Hellenic male ideal, nuns, a traditional bride, military officers; hers by animals, a faun, women of all kinds. These images I have collaged onto the painting from magazine images.

Only in the last panel, after their union, do they actually relate to one another. The male face is softened; he sits on the bench in the moonlight, her element, attending to her wisdom. The feminine figure never changes in any of the three paintings, unlike the man, who undergoes a dramatic transformation. She wears the mask of instinct, a lizard head, and retains her sacred nudity. I recognize these images as an internal drama. The ego part is pictured in relation to the soul. Direction must come from the soul, which is eternal, elemental, and ultimately unknowable to both men and women.

I finished these images and exhibited them in a show on the theme of "Perception of the 'Other' " organized by the Women's Caucus for Art in Chicago. I also organized a workshop with several other art therapists, Rosalind Wilcox, Dollie Hinch, and Rosemarie Conway, on this topic. We all had work in the show and were moved by the concept of the theme, that through art making we could examine our ideas of differentness, otherness. We presented our own artwork and our ideas to the group. We had participants make a self-portrait as a starting point. Then we had participants pair up and first interview and later draw their partner, as well as create a second self-portrait. We then shared the results. All of the participants found the tasks challenging and remarked that the drawing of the portrait as well as being drawn created a sense of intimacy and "knowing" that was quite significant.

I found that my second self-portrait was dramatically different from the first. My initial self-portrait was intended to show different strands of my self. Instead, it came out looking tattered and torn, reflecting difficulties I was having in my new job. I felt depleted and betrayed in a situation I had hoped would be a professionally sound one. In the workshop I became aware of how tired I was of being the "expert," the one in charge. My partner was Peggy Schwartz, an art therapist and former student of mine. She drew a portrait of me that I found very comforting. I felt seen and affirmed in my "ordinariness," rather than valued in my role as teacher or supervisor. Peggy shared that as a student she had admired me but had since developed her own leadership skills and professional identity and so was freer now to see me as a colleague. I had never before realized the price of being a "role model." Admiration of students is very nice but ultimately makes it harder to share or acknowledge feelings that might run counter to the image of competency and professionalism that students rely on while creating their own professional self. By the time I made my final self-portrait, I felt replenished and renewed. Peggy's work had helped me see how embattled I felt with my present students and the toll being exacted. The self-portrait also suggested to me my ambivalence about being open. The paper doesn't quite contain the figure, as if I am worried that my needs, if I really acknowledge them, will be too much.

The work elicited by the image of the Creatrix has been pivotal in my life, marking an acceptance of the creative force within as a worthy guide. The "Perception of the 'Other'" workshop was an exciting attempt to be more fully myself in my work, allowing the work to arise out of real concerns without having a specific goal in mind. It also marked the beginning of truly collaborative work and an new ability to bring my work more comfortably into a public forum. This freedom and sense of following my intuition in my art and life continue to develop.

If you have found the witness relationship successful, consider moving more fully into a co-creative relationship. Using the tasks from the "Perception of the 'Other' " workshop, ask a partner to join you for some art-making time. Your intention can be to enlarge your view of yourself by receiving the perception of the witness. First, each of you create a self-portrait. It can be realistic or symbolic. Share these together, using the witness method you have evolved. Next, draw each other. Take turns so that one person sits while the other one draws. This is another powerful form of witness. When both drawings are complete, share again. Notice what comes up. How is drawing different from simply being together? What do you see about the person that you haven't seen before? Finally, each person creates one more self-portrait in any medium or form you wish.

Each person may spend a brief time with his or her three images, silently observing. Then, hang up all six images together. Sit silently together before all your images. Notice where each of you began. How were you changed by drawing someone else? How was your self-perception changed by being drawn? This process invites the creative energy of the feminine to work in the relationship. From these images, a more genuine awareness of the interconnectedness of all of us can emerge. You can begin to see how interdependent you are on the perceptions mirrored back from others, how a compassionate perception can bring healing. See where your images lead you. Are there ongoing ways to be co-creative in your relationship?

23

Knowing Transformation

My students are drawing storms, practice in the visual metaphor of expressing strong feelings. They are a stormy group, and I feel the brunt of their tumult. I tear off a length of brown paper and decide to join them. First I draw a boundary within the edges of the paper, as if this storm might go off the page. Around me students are becoming smeary with charcoal and chalk pastels. I carefully sketch in a thin, bright horizon line and then fill the upper half of the paper with angry thunderheads. The midground is burnt sienna, and then in the foreground, flames erupt. This is not just a storm but a firestorm, angry and unstoppable. I like the image and take it home.

I stretch a canvas, intending to do an oil painting of the storm. I paint in a strong sky and the earthy ground divided by the thin, bright horizon line. The painting sits on the easel, expectantly, like a stage set. I try to put in the thunderheads, but they look like bowling balls. Adina walks in and says, "Mom, the storm is over." It seems she is right. Somewhere inside of me the thunderheads have given way to rain, which quenches the fire.

I paint in a brown cross on the left, which stands there for days. I think maybe this element finishes the painting, but no such luck. I do some sketches for a crucifixion, in acrylic paint on cardboard. It is the old trickster, my inner masculine, yelling heavenward and bargaining still. He has lost his wings, and his halo lies on the ground. He's emaciated, but actually still quite alive. He has been found out, since the painting of him and his kneeling female supplicant (fig. 13 on page 101), I have been waiting for him to die off and get out of the way. I try to sketch him dead. Then I begin to paint him dead on the cross.

The painting sits and sits. I think about a woman with a hammer in her hand going up to the cross to finish him off. I sketch her and then paint her into the piece going toward the cross with a hammer in her hand. Her hair is writhing snakes, she is powerful, she'll nail him up for good and let the feminine take over. After I paint her in, I realize, he's already been "nailed," so the woman must have some other purpose.

I dream of a witch:

I am with a man. He is strong and handsome. We are at the door of the witch's magic shop. My companion wants to steal some tricks from her. I say this is dangerous. He is very sure of himself. I know she cannot be approached directly. He strides up to the door, which is like a school building door, with wire-reinforced glass in it. He peers inside. The witch sees him. Her eyes are red and protrude from the sockets like snails. When their eyes meet, he flies through the glass. She captures him; he is completely under her power.

In active imagination, I take the dream onward:

I see that I must rescue him by bringing him a silver hand mirror. I sneak quietly into the room, being sure to stay out of the witch's direct gaze. I know she can only be approached from the side. The two of them are crouched down on the floor together. I stand behind her at a little distance and hold the mirror so that my companion can see himself; he has the same red eyes as the witch now. When he sees himself in the mirror, the spell is broken. I stand and hand him the mirror and say, "Hold it to her face." Instead, he hits her with it. She is enraged and curls her bony hand around his ankle as he tries to leave. I say again, "Hold the mirror to her face." This time he does so. As she sees her reflection, she lets go of his ankle to grab for the shiny silver mirror. I touch his hand and we fly out the window, leaving the witch enchanted with her own reflection.

I sketch the witch on cardboard. She is a withered hag entranced with her own reflection. She is the shadow side of the feminine who preys on others. She is what women become when our creativity is denied: vain, ravenous, consuming, living through others. I feel her as a warning to me to nurture my own creativity.

When I put her into the painting, she becomes Kali. In a swirling cloud she emerges as the Dark Mother, who is the last resort of the Devi in Hindu mythology, called forth when change is resisted.

Looking at the painting, I notice that the young woman's legs are not quite right; they seem static. In bodywork I try out the pose of the figure and try to move, and realize that because of the position of the feet, she is stuck. I change the legs so that I lead with the left and am able to move forward in a rocking motion. When I get home, I paint out the lower half of her figure on the large painting and get Adina to pose for me and make the legs striding forward. With that change, I realize that her mission is to take the figure down off the cross. The hammer has two sides and she will use the claw to remove the nails.

I sculpt a dying man in the lap of the woman. She tenderly cradles the too-big head as the body relaxes and sinks back into the earth (fig. 31). Can I really let old roles go and dissolve? What will be left of me? Yet the tenderness of the sculpture reassures me at the same time.

Then, while relaxing in the sauna one day, a vision appears to me of a little baby carried in a blanket by four black birds. He carries a ball of glowing light. I sketch this image and then paint it into the upper right-hand corner of the piece. It stays this way for months. I want it done and off the easel, but it's not ready to go. I get a friend to build a wide frame, but the painting feels suffocated in it. It refuses the boundaries. A male artist friend wonders how I will ever "resolve" the tension in the painting. I show the slide at a gathering of artists, and a woman says, "Why do you have to resolve the tension? Put the painting on top of the frame." This works very well. The vision extends beyond the boundaries of the picture frame, an artificial device that feels confining (fig. 32). These are not merely symbols but the stuff of which my life is made, as real to me as my husband, my child, myself. The tension is ever there, the wheel of

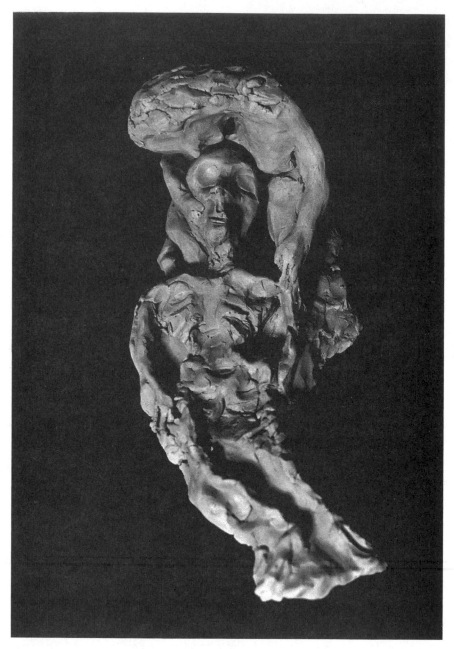

Fig. 31. Death of the Ego *(clay)*.

Fig. 32. Wheel of Life *(oil painting).*

life turning imperceptibly. When I am mindful, and when I am not, the river flows ever onward inside me.

The painting holds the opposites, life and death, new and old, masculine and feminine. It feels like a summation to me, a recapitulation of the themes that have threaded through my life. There is a reason I've had this take-charge, rather cynical and conniving male-identified ego. He has served to help me survive. But I am trying to get his influence in perspective, move toward creative work in a more committed way. All he knows is strategy and manipulation. If it were up to him, I'd stay in academia, stay important, a big talker. He has it all figured out. The feminine has grown conscious enough in me by now that this aspect doesn't so easily push me off balance.

I have also needed to learn about the dark power of the feminine. In Hindu myth, when the Devi, or Goddess, is faced with intransigent power in the figure of powerful male adversaries, Kali appears to break the deadlock. She carries several of her traditional weapons: the scythelike harpe with its curved blade, which symbolizes the indirect way of the feminine, the cutting down that is the harvest; but also the sword with its straight blade symbolizing the path of direct action, sacrifice. She embodies all opposites. Kali takes back all life forms, which she has created, in their due season. She is sometimes shown devouring her own children to express the mystery of return. Kali also holds the snake, another symbol of renewal and continuity, in its skin-shedding ability. She is a strong figure, and I enjoy painting her with all her gory attributes. She makes us ready for fertile emptiness, something I have at times feared and avoided. When I painted Kali, the old woman of the dream was restored to her divinity.

The young woman is an exciting figure of strength and determination. The clay sculpture reveals and clarifies her true purpose: the development of compassion. By attending to the dying figure, she teaches me compassion for myself and my own internal process of change as well as compassion for others. She is a worthy figure, and I feel comfortable identifying with her. My daughter proudly tells friends that she posed for the figure, and I hope to pass the sense of feminine strength on to her.

The baby is the new energy that comes as the old dies. The baby with its glowing light suggests to me that my next work, whatever form it takes, will bring light with it. The birds, which once, long ago, signified death in my early painting with Naumburg, now come as bearers of new life.

Up to this point my work with images has been like feeling my way in a dark cave. I have followed an underground stream that snakes its way beneath my daily life. I lose my way at times, and I have attempted to direct and control this river. I have wanted it to be straighter and more sensible. I have wanted to call it "being an art therapist" or "being an artist." I have wanted to know what is going to happen and have it be simpler. Of course, none of that has occurred.

My image making, I have finally concluded, is primarily an act of remembrance. It is my means to stay in touch with the divine in me. To remember is to re-call, to call back to one's self what was once central but has for various reasons been obscured. It is to re-member, to return arms and legs to one's divine nature by taking back and owning all parts of ourselves. The more of our self we own, the less our need for enemies to embody our disowned darkness. Everything is welcomed by the soul.

Image making always holds out a paradox. Initially, I discovered how dead I really was, and then how much more alive I could be. I longed for that aliveness and the spontaneity and creativity that go with it. The price I paid was that the mirror held up to me by my images showed me my fears, my anger, my rigid and incomplete ego self. To gain life, my "self" as I knew it had to be dismantled. I had to learn to let go of certain dearly held self-images. The rigid self holds not only fear at bay but also love and joy.

I have made the image process integral to my life so that it is a source of constant transformation. Fear is not absent but instead has a place to be expressed. I trust the process of image making so thoroughly as being the voice of inner wisdom that even fear is tolerable, as an aspect of something much larger. The larger something I refer to as the river, it turns out, is life itself, in all its flow, power, unpredictability, shallow parts, and white-water passages. I know now that images will reliably get me into the flow and keep me from getting stuck hanging onto the rotted pilings of self-delusions any longer than necessary. I also trust that the river will not drown me. My job is to stay awake and follow the feelings into the studio.

24

Knowing Nothing

If you allow it to, the image process will weave you like a bright thread through your inner personal world and back again into the fabric of life. Periodically, images may come that seem to summarize your work, your archetypal struggles, as figure 32 did for me. These can be joyous interludes and with them can come, briefly, the illusion of having everything "all figured out." This will pass. Such images do deserve a place of honor and our gratitude. But be aware that the energy within us is alive and playful: it will constantly form and fall apart and re-form into new configurations, new imagery.

A transitional task that sometimes prolongs the sense of peace that comes at a summation time is the mandala. The mandala is a circular drawing that symbolizes wholeness. Although drawing one will not magically render you whole, it is a way of stating intention, and it focuses attention while letting the mind rest. Spontaneous mandalas should be treated like any other image—witnessed and respected. These designs are similar in a modest way to the Tibetan sand paintings, a form of meditation that serves to order inner chaos.

Playing peaceful music and lighting incense or a scented candle helps create the quality of quiet reflection that the mandala drawing fosters. Your intention can be to experience the completion of something or to contemplate the wholeness implied by the mandala.

Draw a circle. Make it large enough to give room for possibility. Either free-hand or using a ruler, divide the circle into sections, using lines, curves, or whatever forms are pleasing to you. Choose a color scheme and literally fill the spaces of your design. You needn't plan the entire piece but rather let it emerge as you go along. I have found

Fig. 33. Mandala *(gouache).*

this an enormously calming task (fig. 33) and also useful at moments when the image work feels dead or a bit chaotic.

If, instead of becoming peaceful, you find yourself enervated at some point in your image-making process, if everything seems like old hat and not much of a challenge, it may be time to seek out a more challenging art process. If you liked sculpture, take a class in stone carving or welding. If painting is satisfying, try classical water-color or sumi brush painting. By placing yourself in the freshness and discomfort of what Zen calls "beginner's mind," you will regain the sense of risk and challenge.

You can also turn your skills outward and use the art process to explore a social issue, as a form of research. What are some images of the abortion debate? Of homelessness? What issues do you want to know about and understand better? Gather media images. Sketch from life. Go to a different part of town than you usually frequent. Open your eyes, open your mind. Art is a way of knowing.

Conclusion

25

Knowing Something

Over twenty years or so I have learned certain truths about image making. Some are probably universal, and then there is content, which is universal in its broad outlines but filled in with my particular details. What I know is as follows.

Reality is simultaneous. Images reveal that we are holographic creatures, living multiple stories. We often get stuck in one view of self and lose the richness of our multiplicity. With this we also lose flexibility, spontaneity, and creativity. We manifest our inner conflicts as blockages in our outward life. For me, work seems to be the primary arena when my conflicts get expressed.

Fear distorts. Fear distorts our vision of the world, so images often manifest initially in very scary forms. I think of the image as being stuffed down into the bottom of a dark closet. When it first comes out, it is all wrinkled and strange. This doesn't make it bad or "sick," just unfamiliar. Getting the image into a form and witnessing it begin the process of undoing distortions.

Intention empowers. Having a clear intention of what we are seeking to know, even in a general way, makes the image process more effective. An intention can be stated in words, but it also needs action in order to manifest. Intention can be general, like "I want to know the meaning of this image," or specific, like "I want to explore my relationship to my parent. It can be simple (the intention to experience paint) or complex (the intention to understand your fears).

Attention transforms. Making the image and living with it, with no other intervention, no assessment, no interpretation, catalyzes change and movement. When the image isn't squashed down in the closet, life returns to flow through it. Attention honors the image and begins the process of reclaiming whatever it represents.

Insight is not change. Insight can be a prelude to change. Images may foster insight or may be totally mysterious. Insight or conscious "knowing"—that is, ideas of what something means—are not necessary for change and don't guarantee change. Another way to say this is that there is usually a long interval between realization and actualization.

Images are patterns. We tend to repeat certain life scenes. Everyone has his or her own repertoire of images, which I think of as the hand of cards we've been dealt. These are what we have to work with. We then arrange the cards in familiar patterns. We all have certain fears to overcome, certain self-aspects that need nurturing in order to balance and move toward wholeness, certain myths and stories that we must live out, certain truths to offer. Getting to know our cards lets us consider new arrangements or patterns.

Patterns are universal. Besides the strictly personal level, there are image patterns that are shared by groups, cultures, and individuals who have had similar experiences. So images provide people with a means to communicate on a deep level with one another. Images of grief will strike a chord in nearly anyone who has mourned a loss, for example.

Images are predictive. Images show what is going on in our inner life. The outward manifestation of what the image represents may not be apparent until long after the image appears. In this way, an image is a signpost and points us in a direction. If we can read the sign, we have a better chance of staying on our own genuine path.

Images need a witness. Image work, at bottom, is about bearing witness to our stories and the stories of others without whitewash or turning away. The witness receives and affirms the ever-changing, ever-evolving story. We are each our own primary witness, and we need to be witnesses for one another. The witness aspect of us is the clear, universal consciousness that underlies our physical manifestation.

Anyone can do this. The image process is available to anyone willing to take up a pencil or paintbrush or lump of clay. Teachers, therapists, guides both inner and outer, and fellow travelers may appear on the path, but image making is ultimately a means of direct knowledge that doesn't require an intermediary.

It is in the telling and retelling, as truthfully as we can, and in the genuine witnessing of all the stories of all people that we heal ourselves and the world. The specific content of my images has so far had to do with receiving the feminine and holding, as best I can, the union of opposites. One of the things that working regularly with images does is challenge my everyday notions of time and space. Life begins to seem more and more like a painting that develops all over in different unpredictable ways, as well as a chronological unfolding of milestones.

At this point certain images have taken on the quality of a lifeline, what geologists call the crack in a cave through which water seeps to create mineral formations deep within the open spaces beneath the earth. The images have a life of their own that has built up slowly over time. I witness and give form to them and attempt to learn what they have to teach.

In order to do this work I have to create situations for it to happen. Like the caves that exist under the earth, I have spaces within me that need to be explored. I must make time and opportunity in my life for image work. I hang the images on the walls of my home. I talk about them with those I trust. Images have taught me and continue to teach me what it means to be human and alive.

Your images are unique and important and belong to the world, for you know something the world needs. The knowledge that comes through your images cannot arrive in any other way. What are you waiting for?

Bibliography

REFERENCES

Adamson, Edward. 1984. *Art as Healing*. London: Nicholas Hays.

Ault, Robert. Undated. "Psycholological Dimensions of Layton Type Contour Drawings." Unpublished workshop handout.

Cane, Florence. 1951. *The Artist in Each of Us*. New York: Pantheon.

Gablik, Suzi. 1991. *The Reenchantment of Art*. London: Thames and Hudson.

Hollander, K. 1993. "Art Asylum." *Art in America*. June.

Hunt, Kari, and Bernice Wells Carlson. 1961. *Masks and Mask Makers*. Nashville: Abingdon.

Kramer, Edith. 1958. *Art Therapy in a Children's Community*. Springfield, Ill.: Charles Thomas.

———. 1971. *Art as Therapy with Children*. New York: Schocken.

———. 1979. *Childhood and Art Therapy*. New York: Schocken.

Macy, Joanna. 1983. *Despair and Personal Power in the Nuclear Age*. Philadelphia: New Society Publishers.

McNiff, Shaun. 1981. *The Arts and Psychotherapy*. Springfield, Ill.: Charles Thomas.

———. 1989. *A Depth Psychology of Art*. Springfield, Ill.: Charles Thomas.

——— 1992. *Art as Medicine*. Boston: Shambhala Publications.

Naumburg, Margaret. 1966. *Dynamically Oriented Art Therapy*. New York: Grune and Stratton.

Mid-America Arts Alliance. 1984. *Through the Looking Glass: Drawings of Elizabeth Layton*. Kansas City, Kans.: MAAA.

Schaefer-Simmern, Henry. 1948. *The Unfolding of Artistic Activity*. Berkeley: University of California Press.

Siegel, Bernice. 1986. *Love, Medicine, and Miracles*. New York: Harpers.

Ulman, Elinor and Dachinger, Penny. 1975. *Art Therapy: Theory and Practice*. New York: Schocken.

SUGGESTED READING

Arrien, Angeles. 1992. *Signs of Life*. Sonoma, Calif.: Arcus Publishing Co.

Edwards, Betty. 1979. *Drawing on the Right Side of the Brain*. Los Angeles: Jeremy Tarcher.

Franck, Frederick. 1973. *The Zen of Seeing*. New York: Alfred A. Knopf.

Gendlin, Eugene. 1978. *Focusing*. New York: Bantam New Age.

Guggenbühl-Craig, Adolf. 1979. *Power in the Helping Professions*. Dallas: Spring Publications.

Hannah, Barbara. 1981. *Encounters with the Soul: Active Imagination as Developed by C. G. Jung*. Boston: Sigo Press.

Johnson, Robert A. 1991. *Owning Your Own Shadow*. San Francisco: Harper.

Jung, Carl. 1979. *Word and Image*. Princeton, N.J.: Princeton University Press.

Nicolaides, Kimon. 1941. *The Natural Way to Draw*. Boston: Houghton Mifflin.

Olsen, Andrea. 1991. *BodyStories: A Guide to Experiential Anatomy*. Barrytown, N.Y.: Station Hill Press.

Watkins, Mary, 1984. *Waking Dreams*. Dallas: Spring Publications.

Resources

ART SUPPLIES

An enormous range of school and artist-quality materials is available from the following company, at two locations and conveniently by mail through catalogue sales.

NASCO Arts and Crafts
901 Janesville Ave.
Fort Atkinson, WI 53538-0901
(414) 563-2446

NASCO Arts and Crafts
1524 Princeton Ave.
Modesto, CA 95352-3837
(209) 529-6957

Daniel Smith, Inc., is another company with excellent-quality materials and frequent sales. Their catalogue, which comes out several times a year, also has instructive essays on materials and techniques.

Daniel Smith, Inc.
4159 First Avenue South
P.O. Box 84268
Seattle, WA 98124-5568
(800) 426-7923

MUSIC

In choosing music to combine with image making, each person must find what is enjoyable and effective. My own predilection to focus on words can be distracting while making art and causes me to choose instrumental music almost exclusively. I find my own tastes run in three basic categories:

percussion; flute and strings, which I find soothing; and world music, that is, recordings from other cultures using instruments and conventions that I am less familiar with.

A good mail-order source for recordings on tape or CD follows:

Ladyslipper Catalogue
P.O. Box 3124-R
Durham, NC 27715
(919) 683-1570

WORKSHOPS

Pat Allen is available to give workshops based on the material presented in this book. She travels frequently to present this work and also gives workshops at Studio Pardes, 350 Harrison St., Oak Park, IL 60304 (708)386-8927. She can also be reached via e-mail at patallen@mediaone.net. Pat welcomes correspondence from readers about their experience with the methods described in *Art Is a Way of Knowing*. Contact her at Studio Pardes.